The Maturing Sun

Angela Bolton

The Maturing Sun

An Army Nurse in India, 1942–45

Imperial War Museum

Published by the Imperial War Museum, Lambeth Road, London SE1 6HZ

Copyright © Angela Bolton 1986
Foreword and Introduction © Trustees of the Imperial War Museum 1986

Dust jacket illustration by David Gentleman

Designed by Herbert Spencer
Printed in Great Britain by
BAS Printers Limited, Over Wallop, Stockbridge, Hants SO20 8JD
Bound by Hunter & Foulis Limited, McDonald Road, Edinburgh EH7 4NP

Maps by Tracey Johnson

Photographs (page numbers):
Angela Bolton Frontispiece, 17, 23, 27, 33, 37, 57, 68, 69, 75, 79, 84, 99,
    103, 107, 115, 120, 139, 154, 155, 159, 166, 169, 175, 176, 180, 196, 202,
    207, 209
Imperial War Museum 50, 55, 59, 113, 153, 163, 185
Imperial War Museum (Cecil Beaton collection) 65, 89, 93, 97
Dr Nicholas Bennett-Jones 124
Bob Sims 135
US Coastguard 45

Frontispiece: The author in 1943

Contents

Page 7   Foreword

8   Introduction

10   *Map of India and Burma*

12   Author's Note

13   1 · A Nurse in the Making

43   2 · Into the Unknown

73   3 · Bengal Posting

110   *Map of Eastern India*

111   4 · Enemy at the Gates

145   5 · On the River

183   6 · End of an Era

215   Index

For my children and grandchildren

Foreword

Although this is the eighth volume in the Imperial War Museum series of personal experience accounts it is the first to be written by a woman. Inevitably most first hand accounts of warfare are provided by men who have fought in battle, but it is part of the Museum's role to collect and preserve the memory of all aspects of conflict. However brave the individual soldier may be, the waging of war ultimately depends upon the quantity and quality of the support services. No one can doubt the importance of the medical services in war nor the dedication and bravery of those who served in them. Angela Bolton's account, written with a lightness of touch and an eye for atmospheric detail, serves to remind us of the invaluable work of many thousands of nurses on all fronts during the Second World War. It also provides a vivid and engaging picture of India, with a number of memorable characters and incidents.

I hope that readers of this book will be encouraged to donate documents and other items relating to conflict in this century to the Museum. We are always anxious to add new material to our collections so that this and future generations may be able to gain as complete a picture as possible of the nature of war. Even though we can only publish very few accounts such as this, our archives are open to all and are widely used.

It remains for me to express my gratitude to my colleagues in the Museum, notably Dr Christopher Dowling and Mrs Jan Mihell, who have nursed the book from manuscript to final production. They have clearly bestowed as much care on it as Angela Bolton did on her patients.

Alan Borg, Director
Imperial War Museum
May 1986

Introduction

The members of Queen Alexandra's Imperial Military Nursing Service (now Queen Alexandra's Royal Army Nursing Corps) played a vital role tending sick and wounded soldiers in every theatre of the Second World War. Two hundred and twenty died on active service, most of them as a result of enemy action. Formed in 1902, the QAs, as they were universally known, had a tradition of skill, courage and dedication stretching back to Florence Nightingale, whose pioneering work in the filthy and fever-ridden hospitals of the Crimea laid the foundations of modern army nursing.

Angela Bolton (then Angela Noblet) joined the QAIMNS in 1941 as a reserve sister after training at hospitals on Merseyside and in Manchester. In February 1942, never having been abroad before, she was posted to India. She arrived at a time of crisis. The Japanese had invaded Burma and the capital, Rangoon, was already in their hands. By May they had swept the British out of the country, inflicting on them a defeat almost as humiliating as the earlier loss of Singapore and carrying the war to the gates of India. For the next two years the Japanese were content to consolidate their position on India's north-east frontier, easily repulsing a British attempt to seize the port of Akyab on the Arakan coast. In March 1944 they launched an attack on Assam with the object both of forestalling a projected British offensive and of exploiting political unrest in the Raj. After eight weeks of bitter fighting around Imphal and Kohima, during which many units were cut off and had to be supplied by air, the British Fourteenth Army under General Slim forced the Japanese into a disastrous retreat. Towards the end of the year the Fourteenth Army crossed the Chindwin. The recapture of Rangoon in May 1945 brought the Burma campaign to a brilliantly successful conclusion.

Throughout this period Angel Bolton served in military hospitals and river steamers in Bengal and Assam (the operational area of the Burma campaign), nursing British, Indian, West African, Chinese, American and even Japanese casualties. Despite long hours of ward duty, often in oppressive heat, she managed to find the energy to keep a diary, on which *The Maturing Sun* is based. As she soon discovered, Burma was one of the most unhealthy theatres of the war, with a formidably high incidence of disease. In May 1943, for every wounded soldier admitted to hospital, there were 120 sick, the majority suffering from malaria. The mosquito was in fact a greater enemy than the Japanese. The annual malaria rate was running at 84 per cent of the Fourteenth Army's strength, though dysentery and scrub typhus also took their toll. At the same time there was an acute shortage of medical officers, nurses and equipment.

Vigorous steps were taken to overcome these problems. The latest medical research was introduced to combat tropical diseases, malaria cases were treated in forward units instead of being transported to base hospitals, an efficient system of air evacuation was organised and preventive measures were strictly enforced. By the end of the war the proportion of sick to wounded had fallen to six to one and the malaria rate to a mere 13 per cent. By ensuring that Slim had the largest possible number of troops fit for front-line duties Angela Bolton and her medical and nursing colleagues made a major contribution to the final defeat of the Japanese, whose own medical services were woefully deficient.

As with the two previous titles in the series, I have to thank my colleague Janet Mihell for her invaluable help in the preparation of this book.

Christopher Dowling
Keeper of the Department of Museum Services

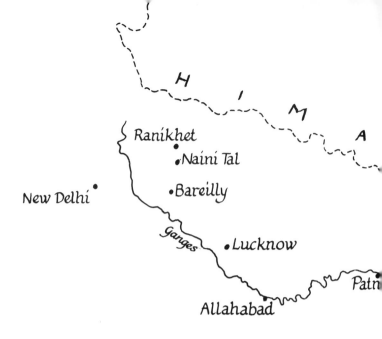

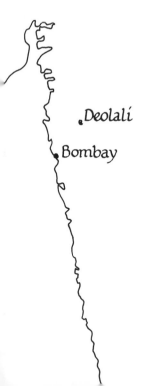

H I M A

Ranikhet

Naini Tal

New Delhi

Bareilly

Ganges

Lucknow

Patn

Allahabad

Ranch

I N D I A

Nagpur

Deolali

Bombay

TIBET

CHINA

H   I   M   A   L   A   Y   A

KANCHENJUNGA

SIKKIM

Darjeeling   •Kalimpong

Dhubri

Brahmaputra

NAGA HILLS

•Gauhati

Shillong   Kohima

MANIPUR HILLS

Silchar   •Imphal

Chindwin

Dacca

•Comilla

Asansol

Chittagong

CHIN
HILLS

Howrah•Calcutta
Budge-Budge

BURMA

ARAKAN

BAY of BENGAL

Irrawaddy

Gopalpur

Rangoon

India and Burma

Author's Note

Four small, battered diaries written in pencil or pen and ink – there were no biros during the war – made possible the writing of this book. One of them measures only three-and-a-half inches by two, for the smaller the diary the easier it was to conceal in my uniform pocket. Obviously they served merely as *aide-mémoires*.

On my free days I would write up anything of interest on scraps of paper so that on my return to England I was able to produce a concentrated account of the war years for my own satisfaction. Thirty-eight years later I responded to an appeal which appeared in one of the Imperial War Museum publications for war journals or diaries. I was encouraged to write a book.

I would like to take this opportunity of thanking all friends and relatives who answered my persistent questions. My gratitude is due also to the library staff of Storrington and Worthing, who went to a great deal of trouble to find references for me.

An account of the 'Forgotten Army' by Major-General Edward Fursdon published in the *Daily Telegraph* has never left my side, keeping me to the straight and narrow path with regard to events that I was not personally involved in.

Finally, the highlight of the whole literary experience has been the intellectual stimulus provided by the association with Dr Christopher Dowling and Mrs Jan Mihell of the Imperial War Museum, who not only edited the book but by a system of questioning drew forth from me memories and reactions that have enriched the narrative considerably. My heartfelt thanks to them both.

1 · A Nurse in the Making

'Faults,' I wrote in my new diary when I was in my sixteenth year. 'Obstinacy. Dislike of criticism. Caring too much about other people's opinions. Ambitions,' – here there was some scratching out and changes of order – 'To travel abroad. To marry a poet. To write a book.'

Whether the faults were corrected in that, or in any other year, it is not my business to say; but the ambitions were fulfilled in the order I finally wrote them down. Clearly I was a very persistent – or a very obstinate – young lady.

The results that I received from my School Certificate examination in the summer of 1935 revealed that I had distinguished myself in the arts subjects but had failed miserably in mathematics. Soon after my seventeenth birthday I left school fully intending to apply for a job on the *Lancashire Daily Post* in order to make a career in journalism.

My father, Thomas Whiteside Noblet, had other ideas. My mother had died when I was thirteen and through being at a boarding-school, the Winckley Square Convent, Preston, I was considered to be 'rather young for my age', which was a way of saying that I was not very worldly-wise. Never having thrown off the attitudes of the Great War, my tall, handsome father informed me that he considered life on a newspaper quite out of the question for any daughter of his – it could mean late nights and little supervision. The best thing for me to do would be to join an establishment as much like boarding-school as possible with a resident mother-substitute – and that meant a hospital.

No one in the family had ever taken up nursing. Those aunts who had a career became schoolteachers, a course closed to me because of my failure in mathematics. I did not want to nurse and told my father so; I said that I wanted to write, reminding him with a certain amount of adolescent complacency that I had always won the school essay competition and that the

13

school magazine would be a shadow of its former self without my prolific poetry. Surely, I pleaded, it was a waste of talent to put me into a practical, down-to-earth job like nursing.

On the contrary, my father argued, it was precisely because my head was in the clouds that I needed to be involved in the practicalities of life. Reasonably enough, he pointed out to me that I could hardly take to writing without experience of some kind, that a hospital offered ample opportunity to encounter human beings at their most authentic and that in the event of a war I would be in a position to observe life – and death – at first hand.

My father said this with feeling. In the Great War, when he was a sergeant with the Royal Garrison Artillery, two fingers of his left hand had been blown off by a German shell. A comrade on the gun with him had been killed outright. It could be conjectured that admiration for the nurses who tended him influenced him in his decision to put me into hospital, as put me he did despite my continuing protests.

My mother's sister, who always took a proprietary interest in her nieces, went to see the matron of the Waterloo and District Hospital, a training school for nurses. This was affiliated to a large Manchester hospital, to which probationers moved in their third year. She learned that there were no vacancies until the New Year and that as I was so young it would be advisable for me to spend the three months' waiting period at the nursing home opposite the hospital in order to get used to the routine.

Half-heartedly I responded to my aunt's letter inviting me to stay with her for a few weeks before starting my nursing career so that she could accompany me into Liverpool to buy my uniform. My Aunt Madge was full of enthusiasm, scenting a new lease of life ahead for herself now that her three motherless nieces were growing up. She was beginning to get bored with the round of village life – the weekly visit to Southport or Liverpool for shopping; the entertaining of doctors and clergy; and the manipulation of her little bits of property, which at least offered the excitement of a threatened law suit if rents were not forthcoming. Aunt Madge was a small, bouncy woman, over-emotional but hard-headed in business affairs. As she talked, her eyes constantly strayed to the large sideboard mirror, where she watched the movements of her still-winsome face with complacent reflection. She began to see herself as a Nursing Home Matron in smart navy blue with a white floating cap on her head, hob-nobbing with her pet doctor, while her newly-qualified niece scurried round obeying her orders.

But that was definitely the second-best fantasy, the first being the role of Bride's Mother. It was with this ambition in mind that she introduced my sisters and me to a constant stream of totally unsuitable young – and old – men; but when she produced a friend of her husband's with a hearing-aid, whose chief interests were Esperanto and Gregorian chant, with whom I was expected to play chess each evening, I put my foot down, refusing to meet any more of her suitors of whatever age or condition. My aunt was very put out, telling me peevishly that I would end up like my father's sister, an old maid, which to her was a fate very much worse than death.

There was nothing my Aunt Madge liked better than to tuck her arm in that of a favourite niece and make for the railway station of her little seaside village of Formby, from where the steam train huffed and puffed its way along the coast until it reached Southport. There she indulged in a shopping spree, energised by coffee and cream-ices, which were served at the cane tables topped with glass in the Kardomah Coffee House. This was followed by a film matinée (price sixpence) where the criterion of excellence was in direct proportion to the moisture content of my aunt's pocket handkerchief. The next port of call was an elegant tea room on Lord Street which offered a cream tea with wild-strawberry jam to be eaten to the accompaniment of a musical trio. Three ladies of uncertain age, in arty apparel, played the piano, violin and cello, entertaining us with excerpts from musical comedies such as *Bitter Sweet* and always ending with a sprightly rendering of 'In a Monastery Garden' by Ketelby, complete with tolling bells low down on the pianoforte. This I really enjoyed, particularly the cream tea, which I prolonged as far as I was able, hoping to avoid what was to follow.

Without a word of warning, my aunt was liable to turn into the doorway of a sleazy-looking apartment house, leading the way up an ill-lit, uncarpeted stairway to a shabby room at the top. An old crone of a fortune teller with a grubby scarf tying back her elf-locks held her palm out for the obligatory offering of half a crown, which was as much as my aunt put on the plate in church. I was forced to listen to an utterly dreary forecast of the future, interspersed with inane admonitions: 'Beware of a cross-eyed stranger.' 'Do not trust a dark-haired gentleman.' 'You will travel over water' (highly likely with frequent pleasure boats plying the Mersey from Liverpool to New Brighton where some of Aunt Madge's friends lived). I used to think as I sat there in the fusty room, trying not to breathe, that fortune telling could be made into quite an interesting pastime if a modicum of imagination were used – but I suppose the old lady felt that it wasn't worth the effort when people were so easily satisfied.

On the day my aunt took me into Liverpool to buy my uniform she hustled me up to John Lewis's uniform department, after being side-tracked by the sight of a Marina green Bride's Mother's hat in the millinery department. We set about choosing the white aprons and caps, stiffly starched belts, cuffs and collars and black lisle-thread stockings to go with the flat ward shoes that comprised the outfit for a probationer nurse. The dresses, a different colour for each year of progress, were supplied by the hospital and, surprisingly, were made to measure by a seamstress, who showed us the crisp pink and white or blue and white striped material before she made it up.

The same evening, my sister Barbara, who had lived with my aunt for several years, joined me in dressing up in the uniforms in order that we might be photographed for posterity. Following Aunt Madge's instructions, we put on the white headsquares as the ward sisters wore them, instead of pleating them into the butterfly shapes which identified the nurse in training. None of us had any idea about the strict rules that governed the wearing of uniform at every stage of a nurse's life.

When I reported at the nursing home at 8am on 7 October 1935, having struggled for half an hour with pearl button clips on unyielding collar, cuffs and belt, I was met by Sister Guggenheim in the ground floor maternity area. She looked me over and quickly ushered me into the nursery where she gently explained that my cap was not quite right. She proceeded to show me how to fold the finicky gathers with the cap on back to front, then how to hold the pleat with a safety-pin, finally turning the cap round to be secured on the head with a kirby-grip. Later on I shuddered with horror when I realised that I might have gone into the dining-room for breakfast with a ward sister's headgear on and would have been considered to be outside the pale for the rest of my stay.

The nursing home was run by an ancient French order of Augustinian nuns and the nursing was of a very high standard.

The author (left) and her sister Barbara dressed as nurses, Formby, 1935.

Though catering mainly for the well-heeled people who lived in Great Crosby and who could afford the high fees, the home had several rooms where elderly or infirm ladies who liked the convent atmosphere and appreciated the fine French cuisine could settle down for life on payment of a reasonable capital sum.

The food was excellent. Sisters and nurses shared a beautiful dining-room, enjoying the same feathery soufflées, delicate game birds and locally grown asparagus as the patients. The nuns lived a separate life in the convent area, to which they were called away for prayer in response to a bell for twenty minutes three times daily, laying aside their long white duty sleeves and protective aprons. Among the French nuns there was a sprinkling of Irish novices, young and full of high spirits, whose laughter prevented me from becoming too depressed by the chronic-sick or dying patients.

My first month was spent with dear Sister Guggenheim in the maternity unit, where my duties were to wheel new-born babies back and forth between their mothers' rooms and the nursery at feeding times, to sterilise any feeding-bottles and to wash the dainty baby clothes with pure white Castile soap which was gentle on the hands. One afternoon Sister Guggenheim called me into the labour ward. 'Would you like to help me with a mother who is having a baby?' she asked. I agreed enthusiastically, garbing myself in a white gown and mask ready for the fray. But the case had obviously been chosen with a seventeen-year-old in mind; a mature mother was bearing her third child and the birth was quiet and controlled so that I was delighted with the experience and with the energetic baby boy that I was allowed to hold. I was also much moved by this astonishing manifestation of new life, retiring to the sluice to shed a few tears.

My first experience of death was more taxing. One of the nuns called me into a room to help lay out an elderly gentleman whom I had nursed. The sister and I worked in silence saying prayers for the dead man as was the custom. The calm reverence for the body made acceptance easier and I was quite pleased with the way I conducted myself – until the moment came for sister to replace the false teeth in the mouth of the corpse, whereupon I swooned on to the discarded linen. I received little sympathy. Sitting in the wide corridor with my head pressed down on my knees, I heard the surgeon on his way to the operating theatre give an amused chuckle as the sister explained what had happened.

I made a friend of pale, ethereal-looking Dorothy Browne, who had started nursing at the same time as I did. Together we attended the lectures on hygiene and anatomy over at the hospital, while one of the nuns at the nursing home taught us to take temperatures, count respirations and pulse rates and wash patients modestly. Later on we were allowed to assist with post-operative dressings, take out 'easy' stitches wearing protective clothing of gauze masks, rubber gloves and gowns like voluminous night-dresses fastened at the back, and finally we were shown how much a blanket bath and a well-made bed could add to a patient's comfort.

At the end of December the Welsh sister tutor, Miss Hughes, informed the Reverend Mother that there were two vacancies at the Waterloo Hospital for Nurse Browne and me. As I made my last entry in my 1935 diary I noticed the picture on the inside cover. It was of the Tower of London – and no prisoner approaching that gloomy edifice could have felt more trepidation than I did as we crossed the quiet suburban road to the training school where we were to spend the next two years of our lives.

The hospital itself was bright and modern with wards on three floors – males on the ground floor, females in the middle and children at the top. The mortuary was in the basement, the lecture room next to the children's ward, while the operating theatre, the heart of our little universe, suitably occupied the centre of the middle floor. Dorothy Browne and I were familiar with the geography of the building from our earlier visits to the lecture room but we had not yet seen our living quarters. We followed Miss Hughes out of the hospital by the Casualty door with a porter forging ahead carrying our cases in his handcart. A few minutes' walk brought us to a three-storied Victorian building, where we were greeted – or rather accosted – by a hatchet-faced female who appeared to be the housekeeper. She told the porter where to put our bags, then disappeared into the nether regions muttering to herself.

Miss Hughes made no comment but led us round the house tutting at signs of cigarette smoking in the shabby sitting-room on the ground floor. There was no place to make tea nor any access to the neglected garden. Each large bedroom on the first floor was furnished with a dressing-table and mirror, a wardrobe, four hard wooden chairs and four single iron beds, one in each corner. The third floor was for night staff. There were only two bathrooms in the building.

'Lights out at 11pm,' said the sister tutor. 'Permission for late-night passes from matron. No musical instruments or animals allowed – and callers in the sitting-room only. Now change into your uniform and report to me in Casualty.'

Dorothy and I sank down on the beds when Miss Hughes had left, regarding each other despondently, then jumped up guiltily, remembering what a dreadful crime it was for visitors and staff to sit on a bed in hospital because it made it look untidy.

Together we discussed our predicament – the lack of privacy, the dearth of armchairs, the possibility of snoring room mates – then slowly changed into our uniforms, I fingering the familiar sore weal round my neck caused by the starched collars, Dorothy complaining about the uncomfortable flat buttoned shoes. Both of us vowed to buy shoes with heels as soon as we could afford them.

Sister tutor was awaiting us with a sheaf of papers in her hand giving the time of off-duty lectures by her and the resident house surgeon. 'Always stand at attention with your hands behind your back when addressed by a doctor or sister,' she said. 'Never wear jewellery on duty. Take that watch off, nurse – what do you think the top pocket in your dress is for? Remember never to get flustered or run except in the case of fire or severe bleeding. You may buy your Evelyn Pearce *Anatomy* from me second-hand. Now, Nurse Browne, you are on Women's Medical and you, Nurse Noblet,' (turning to me) 'are on Male Surgical.' She indicated the staircase for Dorothy and the ground floor for me.

I was absolutely terrified of walking into a ward full of men but I was determined that they should not think that I was new to hospital life; after all I had spent three months with private patients, some of whom were men – even if they were on the wrong side of seventy. In the event I entered the ward half-hidden by the medicine trolley, keeping well behind the staff nurse, who introduced me to each patient in a matter-of-fact way as she handed out the medicines.

The ward sister, a large-boned, sandy-haired Welshwoman, informed me of the hours of duty: 8am until 8pm, with two hours off duty each day; one half-day free a week and one whole day each month. A duty roster was made out a week ahead, the theory being that we could make plans for our time off; but the shifts were frequently changed at a moment's notice so that we could never be sure of sharing a half-day with our friends or of attending a family wedding or a funeral. This was the cause of much bitterness and resentment amongst the young probationers. It was not necessarily the ward sister's fault as wards were often very short of staff when there was an economy drive by the authorities.

Ours was a voluntary hospital supported by contributions from the local community. A committee of 'Friends', together with Miss McLennan the matron, organised money-making events such as fêtes and dances. But they overstepped themselves when they ordered the probationers out in full uniform and capes to go round all the shops in Waterloo High Street with collecting boxes. We were not consulted as to our willingness to take on this embarrassing task in our off-duty time; we were merely told to get on with it. Most of the people we approached were kind and generous but now and then one came across a disgruntled ex-patient with a chip on his shoulder who would refuse to contribute, complaining in a loud voice about the hospital's shortcomings. I would hurry out of the shop with crimson cheeks and eyes full of tears, keeping my head down as I rushed back to the hospital hoping no one would notice me.

After a week in the hospital, Dorothy Browne gave in her notice. It was that shared bedroom that broke her spirit rather than the nursing conditions. When we came off duty on the first day we found a couple of very tall hefty Irish girls established in two of the beds. As there were no armchairs to sit in, that was the only place to be. They were kind and good-natured, but because they had so much weight to carry round rather lethargic, spending most of their off-duty time in bed. We asked them how they came to be in an English hospital as we had heard that the training in Ireland, particularly in Belfast and Dublin, was of a very high standard. They told us that you had to pay fees there. Many girls found it worthwhile to pay the return fare to England twice a year in order to obtain a free training. Naturally they tended to congregate in the Liverpool area, with the result that the local hospitals were never short of applicants. I discovered that all the other nurses and most of the sisters were Irish. The young probationers were friendly enough but could not easily escape the influence of two quite appalling Irish ward sisters, who set out to break my spirit by a series of aggravations and humiliations – presumably because I was English. One day I was ordered to return to the ward at 11am when I had just sunk into an uneasy sleep after night duty. I was finding it very difficult to get into the habit of sleeping during the day and night duty passed in a daze of tiredness. Thinking that there must be some emergency I rose straightaway and I went over to the ward yawning wearily.

Sister Dolan stood there, blue eyes blazing. 'Nurse, you left a broken thermometer in the jar this morning and did not report it.' I was astonished. 'Sister, I most certainly did not break the thermometer.' 'How dare you lie to me. You will take it to the dispensary and pay for a new one.' Two shillings and sixpence was a lot of money from my salary for a crime I had not committed. I turned on my heel and descended to matron's office, where I burst into tears. Matron listened to my story. She had been carefully chosen by the committee to keep a balance between warring factions of Welsh, Irish and English. She was a Scotswoman.

'Go straight back to bed, nurse. I will speak to Sister Dolan.'

When I reported for duty that night I was left in peace to get on with my work and there was a brand-new thermometer in the pot. I managed to find out from Maura Kearney, my chief ally among the probationers, what had happened during the confrontation between sister and matron. Maura had been standing outside matron's office with yet another broken thermometer when she heard Miss McLennan say, 'Sister, if I ever hear of you getting a young probationer out of bed when she has been on night duty you will be dismissed.' From that time on my persecution grew less and in a way I was tolerated, if not accepted – perhaps because I stood up for myself.

After a few months, when I had got over the feeling of always being hungry because of the long hours of work both physical and mental, I was delighted to find that I had lost my boarding-school puppy fat and was becoming quite slim. Then something else happened that cheered me up considerably. A new English nurse arrived to replace Dorothy Browne. Her name was Anne Richardson. Anne and I shared the same interests and a new life started for both of us. We visited the Walker Art Gallery in Liverpool regularly, took advantage of free tickets for Humperdinck's *Hansel and Gretel* and read every book we could lay hands on, discussing them with enthusiasm afterwards. I had found a friend, so that I was now able to bear the pinpricks of hospital life with equanimity.

Anne was the best nurse I ever came across and all the patients loved her. She was thin, sallow-skinned and plain, with smooth dark hair tied in a knot on her neck; she had a lively mind and a comical turn of phrase. Nothing was too much trouble for her on the wards, which she loved so much that she was always the first on duty and the last off. I was able to tell Anne of the terrors of night duty on the ground-floor ward where I was all alone in charge of twenty-six male patients, some of whom were dying. When one patient did die in the early hours, I went upstairs in search of the night sister – at that time one of the two dreadful Irish sisters – but she was nowhere to be found. Down I came again, creeping in fear past the glass doors

Outside the nurses' home, Waterloo and District Hospital, 1936.
Left to right: Maura Kearney, the author, Anne Richardson.

leading to the road, where I was sure there was a lurking
marauder who would ring the door bell, a summons which
it would be my bounden duty to answer. I never discovered
for certain where Sister Cardell used to disappear to for an hour
or so during the night but I suspected that she was in the house
surgeon's apartments.

Night duty on the larger female ward was the most stressful
three months of my training. Nearly everyone in the private
ward and several patients in the other two wards handed in
a grapefruit for breakfast – at that time a status symbol as grapefruit had only been imported for about ten years. To this day
I avoid preparing a grapefruit if I can. We had no special knives
to make the task easier yet every segment of fruit had to be
freed from the skin or there would be complaints to sister. It
was after midnight before we got round to that particular chore

23

as we were kept occupied from 8pm onwards with hot drinks and temperature-taking, medications which had to be checked by the kindly regular night sister, dressings and back treatments with methylated spirits and talcum powder to prevent bed sores, and bedpan removal by the 'runner', a very junior nurse who assisted on the busiest ward. Finally the flowers were taken out of their vases and placed in a handbasin ready for sister to arrange in the morning. This was my favourite job. If I had any time during the night, I would slip into the bathroom to play with the flowers, revelling in their varied scents, colours, forms and textures, responding to a craving for beauty akin to that of a prisoner deprived of light.

As the time approached for the Preliminary Examination set by the hospital at the end of the first year of training, I began to think of ways and means of obtaining the two-guinea entrance fee. We were paid about £24 a year, which was enough for pocket-money but not enough to buy clothes or take a holiday away from home. The exam fee represented a month's pay. Though the two shillings and sixpence a month which I put into Post Office savings would not nearly cover the amount, I was too proud and independent to ask my father for the money. As I sat in the operating theatre in the small hours searching the newspapers in the hope of finding some competition I could enter, I suddenly saw an announcement in the *Daily Sketch*. 'Holiday Romances! Tell us the story of yours on a postcard,' it advised. 'First prize £2-2-0.'

The trouble was that I hadn't had any holiday romances – or workaday ones either, unless I could count Denis Basil, a twenty-one-year-old appendix patient who had written poems to me and came back to collect the Ovaltine he had left behind in the ward kitchen cupboard at 10pm when he knew I would be on duty. He was a charming, quiet, intelligent young man – though not a very good poet – and I was sure that he would ask me out next time he saw me. But there was no story there so I would have to think of something else. I looked round the operating theatre for inspiration. Then it came to me in a flash. I wrote:

'Whilst on holiday I made friends with a boy. Circumstances permitted us to be together for a few days only and during that time he took me to the theatre. It was a holiday romance, soon forgotten. I took up my duties as a hospital nurse once more. One day, months later, I was sent to wheel a patient into theatre for an operation. It was my holiday boy. We smiled and he said, "Once I took you to the theatre, now you're taking me." The operation was successful. Now the romance is no holiday one.'

I stuck a penny stamp on the postcard, posted it the following morning and promptly forgot all about it until a week later when one of the women patients said to me, 'Is this you, nurse?' There under large headlines which read 'HE TOOK HER TO THE THEATRE; THEN SHE TOOK HIM – FOR AN OPERATION!' was my story. I received the two-guinea prize but when I went to matron to pay my fee she lectured me severely for unprofessional conduct in that I had used the address of the nurses' home when writing to a newspaper. I didn't bother to explain – I had won the necessary money and that was all that mattered. But retribution was to catch up with me from another quarter. My poetic admirer must have seen the article too and thought it was true for he never called on me again.

Life was so exhausting during the two years at Waterloo that I did not manage to keep a diary, but I can remember only too well the mistakes I made and the scrapes I got into. It was in the operating theatre that most crises occurred as the tension was so high and the surgeons so bad-tempered (with improved anaesthetics and life-support systems there is not the same necessity for hurried surgery now) that relief was found in somewhat hysterical laughter if anything unexpected happened.

Our favourite surgeon was Mr Charles Wells. It was fortunate for me that he was operating rather than some of the others when I was sent out of theatre to fetch the 'screen', a piece of wire that was slotted into the operating table with a cloth over it so that a patient who had been given a spinal anaesthetic and was therefore fully conscious could not see what was being done to him. But I had no knowledge of that. The screen to me was the large, lumbering, wooden contraption on wheels that was put round the bed of an ill patient in the ward. Congratulating myself that it wasn't being used at the time, I seized the screen from the women's ward and trundled it before me along the corridor and into the theatre. The clatter of instruments ceased and there was dead silence as I peered anxiously round the corner of my prize like a good dog who has retrieved a ball for its master.

Mr Wells looked up from his job of spreading iodine over the patient's skin. 'What is that, nurse?' 'A screen, sir.' 'Have you sterilised it before bringing it into theatre?' 'No, sir.' A glance round the room by Mr Wells to be sure that everyone was enjoying the joke. 'What method of sterilisation will you use, nurse?' Silence from me. 'Will you pour methylated spirits over it and flame it? Or will you put it in the instrument steriliser and boil it for twenty minutes?' It began to dawn on me that he was pulling my leg. Nervous titters broke out and the senior nurse grabbed me by the wrist and drew me outside. She took me to the anaesthetic room where the genuine article was hanging on the wall. I was grateful for the gauze mask which hid my blushes when I returned with it to the theatre.

My annual fortnight's holiday in the summer of 1937 coincided with the arrival of my younger sister Winefride for a short stay with Aunt Madge, and we three sisters were able to make the most of a spell of fine weather. We walked together to Freshfield shore on a blazing hot day, through the resin-scented pine woods with fat furry caterpillars falling off the trees in the heat and the fine sand almost too hot for bare toes. When we reached Aunt Madge's little wooden shack hidden among the sand hills and smelling of coconuts from the fuel that was used to boil water in the primus stove, we changed into bathing costumes and raced down to the deserted beach, catching our tender feet on the sharp marram grass before plunging gaily into the rough waves.

After the bathe we examined the spent sea-wrack along the tide-line for exotic shells, giving the jellyfish a wide berth, then buried ourselves in the hot sand like turtles, complaining that it got colder the further down we dug. Never did tea, well-laced with condensed milk, taste so delicious as on that day. When we reached the limits of the pine woods on our return, there was the welcome sight of an open cab pulled by a strong-smelling, fly-clouded nag ready to take us back to Formby village in sleepy comfort.

Winefride was already contemplating following me into nursing by the end of that fortnight while Barbara was shortly to become engaged. It was the last holiday that we all spent together for a very long time.

Late in 1937 a new house surgeon arrived at the Waterloo Hospital. We knew that he was Jewish and had left Poland because of the menace of Adolf Hitler, information that turned him into an intriguing figure in everyone's eyes. He was a most charming man who seemed middle-aged to the probationers, though he could not have been more than forty years old. Tall

Left to right: Winefride, Barbara and Angela Noblet on Freshfield shore, Formby, 1937.

and dark-haired with slightly stooping shoulders, his horn-rimmed spectacles framing an anxious frown, he still managed to give the impression that he had been a man of some authority in his own country. As his English was poor, he needed a great deal of help with treatments and prescriptions in the casualty department where he worked.

I wondered how the xenophobic Sister Cardell, who had persecuted me and was now in charge of the out-patients department, would react to the foreign Dr Nowak. To my surprise she went out of her way to be helpful, patiently explaining everything to him. Not only that – she softened in her manner to the patients when he was about and even treated me as a human being, asking what off-duty time I would like. I was puzzled and fascinated by the fact that she was acting very much out of character.

One morning Dr Nowak happened to mention that he had a free day and was looking forward to meeting his fiancée, also a doctor, who had lately arrived from Poland. I watched Sister

Cardell's face change back to its former grim expression. From that moment she started to persecute him in lots of little ways. She also instigated a campaign of denigration against him among the staff so that his life was made more and more difficult and he must surely have felt the enmity around him. I longed to say something comforting to him but I was not sure how he would take it and was afraid that he would consider me to be presumptuous. It was a relief to know that he had the support of his fiancée, who had found a job in a Liverpool hospital where Dr Nowak was able to join her in a more senior position the following year. By that time I had moved on to the children's ward with anxieties of my own to cope with.

It was on this ward, the last one I worked on at Waterloo Hospital, that I broke the rule that nurses must not become emotionally involved with their patients. I was fond of children and it disturbed me when parents were not allowed daily visits to very young or ill patients in case the separation at the end of visiting time caused tears or tantrums. Many children were quite happy when their parents left but others turned their faces to the wall, refusing to eat or sleep. Quietness and order in the ward took precedence over the idosyncracies of children. The cry of the six-year-old girl, brought in too late for a successful operation on an appendix that had already perforated, still rings in my ears, 'I'm going to die! I'm going to die!' And die she did before morning without seeing her parents, as she was unconscious when they arrived. The parents could have been allowed to stay when the prognosis was so bad, but no one appeared to think it necessary. We were not encouraged to play with the children or comfort them. Sister always found something for me to do, such as tidying the medicine cupboard, if she caught me playing with a child.

Into the children's ward one day came Florence May Walter, aged two. Her home was in Scotland Road, the poorest area of Liverpool, where the police went round in pairs but the midwives were safe. She was the last child of a large improvident family with an unemployed father and a downtrodden mother, who seemed only too relieved to leave her child in hospital in order to have one less mouth to feed.

Florence May had sucked her thumb to such an extent that it had become badly infected. She cried continually. She was also dirty, verminous and emaciated. Sister told me to start by giving her a bath and a hair wash. Dressing myself in a rubber apron covered by a towelling one and putting on a cap for fear of head lice, I ran a bath in the warm nursery, then coaxed the child out of her wretched clothes and into the water where she stopped crying in order to play with a rubber duck. When I extracted her from the bath ten minutes later, cuddling her to me in an enveloping towel, I found that her hair was springing up into a mass of golden curls. She sat quietly while I dressed her thumb, then lay peacefully against me in perfect trust. From that moment on I loved Florence May Walter, dreaming of ways to keep her in my care.

Every two hours I fed the little girl until the scrawny body began to show the normal curves of childhood. She had stopped the constant crying but was too listless and withdrawn for the doctor's liking so that he actually told me to play with her, which suited me very well. I knew it was quite crazy, but I planned to adopt Florence May. I approached Aunt Madge to ask her if she would give the child a home if I contributed to her keep. My aunt refused to consider the idea. She was far too old to take on a young child, she said. She asked me how I thought the child's mother would react. Just because home conditions were bad it didn't mean that a child wasn't loved.

I grew desperate as the time drew near for Florence May to go home. She now looked the picture of health, laughing and playing with me, her sore thumb forgotten, but I knew that within a few weeks of leaving us she would drift back into her former state. I even had the temerity to ask the ward sister if anything could be done to help her but she shook her head, pointing out that there were thousands of children in the same situation and that it would be useless to become involved in her life. I made certain that I was off duty on the day that Florence May went home. I could not bear to see her go.

During the second year at the Waterloo and District Hospital those of us who had passed the Preliminary Examination in Anatomy, Physiology, Hygiene and Nursing Care learned to give hypodermic injections, to administer oxygen and carry out a Fractional Test Meal for stomach content analysis. We knew how to persuade patients with pernicious anaemia to swallow the dried extract of hog's stomach and the scraped liver sandwiches which were the treatments for the illness before liver injections came into vogue. We had a good working knowledge of diabetes just fourteen years after Banting had isolated insulin, a discovery that saved the lives of so many young sufferers. Finally, we could take full responsibility for a ward all day so long as there was a sister or doctor in the building. It was time for us to leave the nursery slopes for a more rarefied atmosphere.

Anne Richardson and I, now both nineteen years old, went our separate ways on holiday, arranging to meet a fortnight later at the gates of the hospital with a thousand beds in a Manchester suburb where our final two years of training would be spent.

Crumpsall Hospital was gigantic. Its huge smoke-stained Victorian brick buildings were chained to each other by bridges which formed links between the gaunt three-storey blocks. Each block was identified by a letter of the alphabet from A to E; if you wanted to go to E Block from A you allowed a good five minutes' travelling time. It took us weeks to find our way round to all the departments. I, having no sense of direction whatever, was constantly being rescued from a distant outpost by the hospital porters.

Some of the wards had been modernised by the addition of glass partitions and layers of cream paint but others were dreary indeed, very long and featureless with shiny dark green and brown paint and doors that swung open in the winter gales to allow snow and dead leaves to enter. They must have housed the sick-poor of the last century. Two wide drives served the hospital: one leading from the Crumpsall suburbs straight to the main entrance in A Block with a branch line up to the nurses' home; the other winding half-a-mile through lonely grounds to E Block.

The nurses' home, however, was completely modern with much thought given to the comfort of the staff. The rooms, one for each nurse, were fresh, well-furnished and warm with large windows overlooking staff tennis courts or pleasant grounds. The enormous recreation room was provided with plenty of well-upholstered armchairs and sofas, a grand piano and a Tannoy speaker on the wall which relayed music or news from some centre in the hospital. On each of the three floors was a kitchenette where the planners had envisaged the happy nurses tripping in to make a cup of tea or coffee when off duty. But the heads of the nursing staff had not caught up with the planners: the kitchenettes were out of bounds to nurses. A smart little maid was kept busy making hot drinks for the sisters and 'supers' (superintendents) and between times the doors were kept locked by order of the home sister. The grey-clad supers had an irritating habit of bursting into one's bedroom, using a master key, at every time of day, destroying any illusion of privacy in our lives at the age when we needed to be free from hospital interference.

Anne Richardson and I found ourselves at opposite sides of the two-hundred-roomed nurses' home – about as far apart as we could be. Blackbirds and thrushes scratched busily among the flowering currant bushes outside my window, one particular thrush arriving regularly on my window sill each morning to sing a song that was just like 'Six o'clock, nurse, up you get!' over and over again. In the evenings, from the tennis courts, which were almost completely monopolised by doctors and sisters, came the sound of pattering balls and laughing arguments. I resolved to join the tennis club immediately.

The matron, Annie Burgess, was a severe-looking lady with iron-grey hair and a disposition to match. Because we seldom saw her, except in the distance, we exaggerated her fearsomeness in our minds, hiding in the sluice if we saw her crossing one of the bridges towards our block. A rumour prevailed that if Annie Burgess visited a sick probationer it was a sure sign that that particular nurse was in danger of death. We use to imagine her lurking like an octopus, the supers being her tentacles, endowed with the ability to creep into every corner and crevice of our lives. Four of the five supers were particularly embittered women whose future husbands had been killed in the Great War. Now I can look back with sympathy for them but it was not easy to make allowances when one was at the receiving end of their sarcasm.

We were all very much afraid of the night super, Miss Kenwright, the last of whose duties before going off to bed in the morning was to oversee the day staff's breakfast at 7.30am. If you came in late she was quite capable of sending you out of the dining-room hungry to face several hours of work. Moreover, when doing her ward round at 10pm, she would pause at the bedside of each of the forty patients, expecting you to say, without hesitating, the name, illness and treatment. If you faltered she would turn on you angrily, subjecting you to a public dressing-down.

After a time I discovered that she didn't notice if I got the name or illness wrong so, with the willing connivance of my patients, I hurried her round the ward. 'Mr Brown, fractured femur. Put in plaster with extension. Mr Black, spondylitis deformans. To see consultant tomorrow.' But just when I thought I had the whole thing taped, Miss Kenwright caught me out. I said, 'Mr Green, fractured wrist. Colles' splint applied,' noticing too late that the patient had a 'cage' over his legs to protect a lower limb injury. 'And Potts's fracture of the left ankle,' I added, quickly moving on to the next bed. She gave me an old-fashioned look but said nothing as she swept out of the ward and across the bridge, her apron and veil blowing furiously in the wind.

How the patients enjoyed it all. Plastered limbs waved about at great personal risk; ambulant patients almost fell off their crutches laughing; while the weights on Mr Green's extension oscillated precariously in time with his shaking shoulders.

Miss Kenwright was a heavy woman – we said it was because she ate the breakfasts of the nurses she turned away for being late. Be that as it may, this was the limerick I wrote which was sung for her at the staff concert, where a certain amount of licence was accorded the probationers:

> If when late in the morning you tender
> An excuse that is blatantly slender,
> Miss Ken*wright* knows your tricks
> And like TWO TONS OF BRICKS
> Will come down on the tardy offender.

For the fair-minded super, whom we liked and respected, I wrote:

> Now Miss Spenlowe will give you a break,
> For kindliness she takes the cake.
> She remembers you know,
> When she was a 'Pro'
> What a diff'rence a kind word could make.

'Pro' was an abbreviation for 'probationer' and at the time we didn't know that it had other connotations. We did wonder why the doctors laughed so heartily. Poor, dear Miss Spenlowe. I hope she understood how well-intentioned we were.

Having dealt with acute surgical cases and diseases of the first half of life at the Waterloo Hospital, we were now to gain experience of chronic illnesses and elderly, bedridden patients. It was depressing enough to see the long wards of people who would never get well, but even more depressing was the atmosphere of the vast infirmary that made you feel like a particularly insignificant cog in a Moloch of a machine. Nobody ever praised you for work well done but the slightest mistake or

The author (left) and Maura Kearney on Freshfield shore, 1939.

imperfection was magnified into a serious crime. If you were ill, that was the worst crime of all, the word 'malingering' being bandied about a great deal. There was a sick bay but you had to have something as concrete as an acute appendix before you could be admitted.

The world of politics impinged not at all on our self-contained lives. We hardly noticed when Neville Chamberlain came back from seeing Hitler in Munich waving his piece of paper which, he declared, meant 'peace for our time'. But in the space of a year things looked very different. I was on night duty on 3 September 1939. Instead of going to bed as usual when I had finished, I stayed up to hear the expected statement by the Prime Minister at 11.15am. Day and night staff were gathered together in the recreation room talking quietly as they knitted or skimmed though the pages of *Nursing Illustrated*. There was an air of suppressed excitement as we waited for the crackling of the Tannoy system which preceded an announcement. Big Ben struck the quarter. 'This is London,' came the familiar voice. Then Mr Chamberlain spoke, telling us of our responsibilities towards our Polish allies and of the intransigence of Herr Hitler, who had not replied to his ultimatum. We were at war. Nothing would ever be the same again.

However, as very little happened except for the building of shelters and one false air raid alarm, we returned to our old routine of work and study, almost forgetting about the war. One day I was posted to a very large ward for the elderly, a temporary building like an army hutment, which had been brought into use while their own ward was being modernised and fitted with black-out curtains. It should have been a depressing place to work, with its unending routine of blanket-bathing and changing incontinent patients, but because we were some distance away from the main blocks and had a lively and cheerful young sister in charge the atmosphere was relaxed and enjoyable. Every evening there was a sing-song, in which the patients joined, and there were jokes and laughter that would never have been heard in the main building. No one in authority came near us. The patients claimed that it was like being in one big happy family and not one of them wanted to go back to the old ward.

Although I had signed on for three years' training on reaching the age of eighteen, I was told that I could not take my finals until I was twenty-one. As that birthday came in July 1939, two weeks after the exam, I had to stay on for another six months in order to sit it in December. I felt annoyed and disappointed but my friend Anne Richardson had to face a far worse blow. Anne lived for her work because she found it entirely satisfying but she never became a bore about it, refusing to talk shop when off duty. She was born with a slight cleft palate so that her speech was not quite so clear as other people's, though this made no difference to the patients: they understood her perfectly well and she understood them.

One evening I found Anne lying on her bed crying loudly and desperately. She had been called to the office of Matron Burgess, who had informed her baldly that, because of her 'disability' (the cleft palate) she would not be allowed to take her final exam.

I wanted to storm in on Annie Burgess straight away but Anne begged me to do nothing to antagonise the authorities so near my own finals. She was sure the matron would not change her mind – those in authority in our hospital would be most unlikely to do that as it would mean losing face. There was nothing for it but to help Anne pack and to promise to write to her regularly.[1] I felt very low indeed and furious with the stupid hospital that had let its best nurse go. As the days went by I felt more and more frustrated and dispirited; it was bad enough working in a soulless atmosphere year after year but without friends it became intolerable. Even the thought that the approaching exams would make me a free agent had no power to lift me out of the slough of despond into which I had sunk. In the end I decided to ask for an interview with Matron Burgess though I had not yet formulated in my mind what I would say to her.

With ward sister's permission I left the duty room, rolling down my sleeves and slipping on my starched cuffs as I walked down the corridors to matron's office. A tap on the door, a peremptory 'Come in', and I was confronting the lioness in her den. Before me, protected by a heavy mahogany desk, sat a large full-busted female whose raised eyebrows gave her face a supercilious expression. Though I had seen her on the wards, it was the first time I had been alone with her.

'You asked to see me, nurse?'

'Matron, I wish to be relieved of my contract. I do not feel well enough to finish my training.'

She surveyed me, pen in hand, then deliberately placed the pen in a tray, clasped her hands before her and leaned forward until her bust rested on the desk.

'Nurse, I know that you have lost your friend in the last month or so, but these things happen. Life is not a bed of roses. If you leave without taking your exams you will regret it all your life. You will have wasted four years.'

I stared at her in astonishment. She actually knew who I was and what had happened to me. I was thrown off balance by the unexpected disclosure, forgetting all the accusatory things I meant to face her with.

'Go back to your ward, nurse, and take a rest from your studies for a day or two. I was hoping you would stay on at Crumpsall to take your midwifery training.'

'No thank you, matron,' I muttered as I slid out of the office and walked off down the corridor, going through the old familiar routine of removing my starched cuffs and covering

[1] Anne Richardson was eventually accepted by the Stanley Hospital, Liverpool, and became a state registered nurse.

my rolled-up sleeves with cuffs of ruched cotton.

My interview with Annie Burgess made me realise that it was not the individuals but the system that was at fault, though at that time I was too inexperienced and ignorant to know what steps could be taken to change conditions. Anne used to ask me why I stayed on when I wasn't particularly happy and had no vocation to nurse. The answer was that I could feel it doing me good; no longer was I dreamy, absent-minded and untidy, but capable, efficient and orderly. Secondly, I was observing everything that happened and already weaving it into story form in my head. I might have been unhappy but I was never bored.

As the time of the hospital exams drew near, to be closely followed by the State Finals, a notice went up on the board inviting nursing and medical staff with their friends to a fancy dress ball. Matron, four supers and the chief medical superintendent used to attend these affairs, all of them dancing except matron, whose status was that of a being far too dignified to take to the floor like ordinary mortals. The event was held in the huge recreation room of the nurses' home. It was a brave young man who would come there to dance with that grey-clad phalanx of grim-looking females looking on. Dr Ramsay, a sandy-haired Scotsman, was the chief medical superintendent and the most important person in the hospital – even more important than matron. He put in an appearance at the ball in order to make the supers and sisters happy by taking a turn round the dance floor with them. All eyes were upon him as we seldom had an opportunity of seeing this eminent personage.

For the occasion I had made myself a short rose-coloured tunic of satin and wore my only pair of silk stockings and high-heeled shoes. I had had my fair hair cut in a page-boy bob with a fringe. The hospital had hired a band, which played the usual quicksteps, foxtrots and waltzes. My partner was a callow youth brought in for me by a friend, who trod on my precious shoes all the way round the floor. I ditched him during an interval, dancing rather drearily with other girls for some time; then an 'Excuse me' dance was announced, which was a licence for anyone to approach a couple, tap one of them on the shoulder, say 'Excuse me' and make off with the partner. It was a waltz, 'One Day When We Were Young'. Maura Kearney swept by on the arm of my discarded escort. 'I dare you to excuse Dr-Ramsay!' she squeaked in her high-pitched voice. Dare I? The

Christmas at Crumpsall Hospital, 1939. The author is at the back, on the left.

anger and frustration that had been building up in me for so long made me reckless. It was a challenge; I would strike a blow for the poor and downtrodden of this hospital. I began to weave my way purposefully across the floor.

It was much easier than I expected and the middle-aged Dr Ramsay turned out to be an excellent dancer. 'Who are you supposed to be?' he asked when he had recovered from the shock of being excused by someone who was patently not a sister. 'I'm a page,' I said breathlessly as we whirled round. 'You mean a page out of a book?' 'More or less,' I answered. This led on to a conversation about books in general. After a while we sat out and he brought me refreshments. It would be pleasant to be able to report at this point that I told him all the things that were wrong with his hospital – and indeed I might have done so if there had been anything stronger than lemonade to drink. Just when we were about to take to the floor again everyone stood up to sing 'God Save the King'. It was midnight.

Like Cinderella I fled from the ballroom to seek sanctuary in my room, where I awoke to the cold light of day a few

37

hours later wondering dismally what retribution would follow my foolhardy performance of the previous night. At breakfast the Irish nurses commiserated with me. 'You're for it now, kid. Fancy excusing Sister Kean from theatre. Your own boss! You might at least have waited until he was dancing with a sister from another ward.'

I had to wait all day before facing Sister Kean, which would have given her time to talk things over with matron. When I came on duty at 7pm there was a message for me telling me to report to sister's office. 'Sit down, nurse.' She pretended to be writing a report but I knew she was hoping to prolong the ordeal. After a minute or two of silence, during which I studied her features covertly, failing to find any trace of human sympathy, she looked up to ask silkily, 'Nurse, do you know Dr Ramsay socially?' Clever of them, I thought, she has been told by matron to go carefully. I drew a deep breath. 'Yes, sister,' I said.

Well, it *was* true. I did know him socially – only since last night – but still I certainly knew him socially. A glimmer of an unwilling smile relaxed her thin lips. 'You may go, nurse.' I was safe. They could hardly ask Dr Ramsay how long he had known me. I had done the unthinkable and defied the system. I began to feel happier and went off with assurance to take my final exam.

In the spring of 1940 I at last received my certificate of state registration as a qualified nurse. I would have liked to join one of the nursing services but, realising that I was rather young and inexperienced to take on a sister's responsibilities and being attracted to the tropics rather than the European theatre of war, I decided to apply for a six months' training course in tropical diseases at the Seamen's Hospital in Liverpool, only to discover that it had been closed down for the duration of the war. Nothing daunted, I concluded that a year's training in infectious fevers would be the next best thing, so the summer found me at the Cuddington Isolation Hospital at Banstead in rural Surrey. After working in a suburban hospital, then in an infirmary that served a big city, it was a pleasure to spend a year on the edge of Epsom Downs. On either side of the long lane that led up to the hospital grew blackberry bushes festooned with thousands of scintillating cobwebs which spattered me with dew on my early morning walks before breakfast. Along the grass verges ragwort flourished, host to colonies of curious red and black flies, whose lives appeared to be spent in complicated rituals of courtship. The war seemed very far away.

A solidly built nurses' home stood in the midst of wards of wooden hutments, spaced well apart, for the isolation and treatment of diptheria, scarlet fever and whooping cough. There were single-room wards for sporadic cases of meningitis, poliomyelitis and encephalitis, the rare deaths that occurred being caused by tubercular meningitis, for which there was no known cure. An elderly medical man reeking of stale smoke, who would have been pensioned off had it not been for the shortage of doctors brought about by the war, went round the wards each morning. He would sit down at the desk, sucking on an ancient pipe whose nicotine-stained bubblings shot out all over the case histories, and ask, 'Well, nurse, what'll I put, eh?' We would dictate the details of the patient's condition to him, then remind him of the treatment he usually ordered. I had not much confidence in him as a medical practitioner until I had to call him out in the small hours because a ten-year-old boy with laryngeal diptheria was turning blue. The old man performed a faultless tracheotomy which saved the child's life. 'Haven't done one of those in years,' he chortled, lighting up his disgusting pipe and looking about ten years younger.

I was happy at Banstead, feeling relaxed and peaceful for the first time in five years of training. On a staff nurse's pay, I had no trouble whatever in finding enough money for the infectious fevers exam fee. Despite the strict rationing we did not go hungry, as we were encouraged by the Ministry of Food to 'dig for victory', the vegetables and fruit we grew proving welcome additions to our restricted diet.

I had not been at Cuddington long when the Battle of Britain began to affect our carefree, well-ordered way of life. Now, almost daily, we watched dog fights going on over our heads as the planes of Fighter Command engaged the Luftwaffe in a critical trial of strength. On 15 August in the early evening a whole formation of German bombers passed over the hospital, the distinctive low vibrating hum causing us to dash for shelter in the basement even though there had been no alert. Later we saw them returning in some disarray but it was not until the following day that we heard rumours that Croydon had been bombed in mistake for Kenley fighter station and that the Koh-i-noor pencil factory by the airport had been destroyed. In fact it was Croydon airfield that received the direct hits.

Early in September the Blitz started, bringing the Banstead and Sutton area into the flight path of bombers bound for

London and making it a matter of expediency that the hospital should have an air raid warden to train the staff in fire fighting. Night after night we put the child patients under their cots and beds when the undulating wail of the air raid siren sounded. One small baby with whooping cough used to work his legs in such a way that he slid over the polished floor, being discovered nightly behind the ward door when the sister did her rounds. We had to harness him to the legs of his cot to prevent his noctambulations. To shield us from stray flak as we went on duty, we had the use of an ambulance known as the 'Death Trap', which was open at either end, giving very little protection. Our hospital porter ARP warden drove us round during air raid alerts wearing a steel helmet and protective gauntlets. It was disconcerting to hear the rattle of flak on the roof as we darted from the ambulance to the wards.

We day staff slept on the cement basement floors with our valuables in little boxes under our pillows. One night we were awakened by a loud explosion. An oil bomb had fallen in the field next to the hospital, causing a fire which lit up the wooden hutments of our wards. The German airmen must have thought we were an army barracks for they showered us with incendiaries. Everybody lent a hand in the emergency. Nurses carried buckets of sand, with which the porters smothered the roof-top flames. The ARP warden used a stirrup-pump to put out the incendiary bombs on the ground. The chief clerk, a dashing young man in a siren suit, organised a hose-pipe brigade to carry water to the oil bomb fire over the fence, gradually bringing it under control. We were appreciative of the fire-drill practice we had been given, which was the reason that there were no casualties that night; a few windows were broken but the children slept peacefully through it all under their cots.

Sometimes on night duty I would stand outside the ward gazing upwards, fascinated by the criss-crossing of searchlights in the dark sky. I couldn't help feeling excited when the black shape of a German bomber was outlined in their pencil beams for a few seconds. I could imagine the pilot's feelings as he twisted and turned, frantically trying to escape the probing fingers of light which would reveal his position to the anti-aircraft defenders. Soon all would be dark and still once more, with only the pale gleam of the distant stars winking among the clouds.

My sister Barbara, married at the instigation of Aunt Madge, lived at Wallington, a few stations along the line, where she spent most nights in an air raid shelter. When I visited her I was careful to catch an early train back to Banstead in order to miss the German bombers. We all avoided going up to London if we could, though I did risk it once in order to meet an old school friend, Muriel Wright, who had just finished a degree course at London University. We sat on a park bench in the sunshine catching up on the news of the past five years, steadfastly refusing to acknowledge the presence of two young Canadian lieutenants who paraded back and forth in front of us anxious to cement Anglo-Canadian relations. In the afternoon we went to a matinée of *Sweet and Low*, made memorable by a take-off of *Madam Butterfly* by a foghorn-voiced Hermione Gingold, whose Japanese coiffure was plentifully skewered with knitting-needles embellished with the flags of all nations.

As we walked back to Victoria station along the gap-toothed streets, noting the boards nailed crosswise over the doors and windows of damaged buildings to prevent people entering and disturbing the shaky fabric, a cluster of colourful Very lights, bright as Christmas tree baubles, floated down in the distance. It was difficult to believe that they had any sinister significance but we knew that they were associated with the air battles. It was turning dark when Muriel waved me off on the Banstead train. Huge barrage balloons on the city's perimeter loomed grey and elephantine waiting to entangle enemy aircraft in their tethering wires. There were few passengers about. My cold, empty compartment was only faintly lit by a blue light – just bright enough to see that the routine notice, 'Blinds must be kept down after dark', had been altered to 'Blondes etc etc', by some wag. The journey was depressing and very eerie, being made more alarming by the necessity to count the stops because the names had been removed from the stations.

When I left the ghostly blue-lit Banstead station I had to face the long countrified drive leading up to the hospital. We all carried dim pocket-torches but they only intensified the fear that an assailant would be able to see you more easily whereas he would not be visible. It was a great relief when the tiny lines of light round the ward windows, which the ARP warden would have disapproved of, came into view.

Early in December 1941, after I had taken the exam which made me a state registered fever nurse, I opened a newspaper one day and saw an urgent request for trained nurses to go overseas with the army. This was the summons I had been waiting for and I lost no time in putting in a request for an interview with the charming Queen Alexandra's Imperial Military Nursing Service matron of the Royal Herbert Hospital, Woolwich, who was on the point of retiring. I was asked during our informal chat if I was prepared to go overseas within a few weeks and answered in the affirmative.

One of the last things I did before leaving Banstead was to purchase a Nursing Mirror Diary, for I had already surmised that 1942 would be a memorable year. It had several useful pages on nursing procedures and, because of the war, a large section on 'Principal Gases and their First Aid Treatment', which fortunately I did not need to refer to. Unexpectedly its 'Mohammedan Calendar' came in extremely handy; also there was a paragraph on 'Nursing Homes' which would have been an eye-opener to my Aunt Madge. 'Registration may be refused if the Home is not in the charge of a medical practitioner or a qualified nurse.'

On 15 December 1941, my interview having proved successful, I arrived at the Royal Herbert Hospital just in time to join in the farewell fancy dress party for Matron Bell held in the sisters' mess. I went as a cat, complete with tail and whiskers. A saucer of champagne was put down on the floor for me but the matron's dog beat me to it. We drank the health of Miss Bell, a tall dignified figure in short scarlet cape and grey uniform frock, who to show that she was retiring in full vigour turned a neat somersault on the rug without disturbing a hair of her head – not the sort of thing Annie Burgess of Crumpsall would have done.

It was a splendid evening, the beginning of an era. On Friday 2 January 1942 I wrote in my new diary, 'Bardia taken by the British. Photo taken for my Identity Card ready for going abroad. Nurse Hobley blown out of kitchen, eye-brows singed. (Gas cooker – not bomb.)'

Within a fortnight four of us, all answering to the title of 'sister' for the first time, with temporary commissions in the army, set off for Oxford by train, resplendent in the scarlet and grey outdoor uniform of the Queen Alexandra's Imperial Military Nursing Service (Reserve).

2 · Into the Unknown

Of the three young sisters who had left Woolwich with me to mobilise in Oxford, two were named McKenzie and came from the Highlands of Scotland; the third, a Lowland Scot, had trained at Edinburgh Royal Infirmary. Her name was Doris Oliver, her manner quiet but friendly and the expression in her dark eyes mockingly mischievous. It was she who immediately pointed out that, while we were in the forces, our associates would be those people whose surnames came next to our own in alphabetical order: thus, 'McKenzie, McKenzie, Noblet, Oliver.' There was no hope whatever, she maintained, of being in contact with those whose surnames began with A or Z. I said I thought I would be quite happy with that arrangement and from then on we were friends.

Doris was thin, of medium height with hair of a russet colour waving naturally over her small head. She had a well-shaped slightly aquiline nose with a generous, full-lipped mouth. Her voice was soft and she had a lilting way of speaking that I had never heard before – quite different from the brisker, sharper accents of the two McKenzie girls. By the end of the train journey to Oxford I found myself pronouncing words in a decidedly Scots fashion and had to pull myself up in case they thought I was imitating them deliberately.

We discovered that we had all joined the QAs for the same reason – we had seen the appeal in the newspapers and felt it our duty to respond. Only Dora McKenzie, alert and fierce as a Scots terrier, had been through a baptism of fire as a midwife in the slums of Glasgow. The rest of us were mere tyros.

Once we had settled into our billets at St Hugh's College, we were kept fully occupied in signing for uniform and allowances, ordering steel trunks from All-Kit in the Turl, being inoculated at the Examination Schools and dashing up to Harrods by train for our white tropical uniforms and sola topis. The weather was dreadful. Snow fell heavily on the first day of February, making it difficult to get about. Because of petrol rationing the buses were few and far between but the car drivers of Oxford were very generous with lifts when they saw us in uniform. Before we were sent on a few days' embarkation leave we were warned to leave our trunks ready packed, together with our bedding-rolls, so that we could move off at short notice. The secrecy about the date was to bamboozle the enemy, who was 'always listening' according to the posters on the Post Office walls.

At 5am on 13 February we were told to get up immediately to finish packing and by 8am we were leaving the cold, murky Oxford railway station on a train full to the last seat with army personnel. A few hours later, after the regulation wartime stops and starts, several people recognised the approaches to Liverpool Docks, at which point we detrained to join other sisters in the short march, two by two, on to the decks of the *Monarch of Bermuda*.

There were sixty sisters and about a thousand troops on board by the evening. Three of us shared a pleasant cabin – Margaret Orr, twenty-two years old and the youngest sister on the ship, Doris Oliver and myself. None of us had ever been at sea before and we were full of excitement and youthful anticipation. Margaret sat on the top bunk swinging her long shapely legs and Doris, whose generous-hearted appraisal was salted with a dry humour, told her that those well-shaped limbs would take her a long way out East. They did too – all the way to the Arakan front.

As there was very little floor space in the cabin, we all agreed to keep everything as tidy as possible, then exclaimed with delighted surprise when what we thought was a cupboard turned out to be a modest-sized bathroom. We looked each other over in our smart tailored grey suits with scarlet piping and made our way to the deck with mounting enthusiasm.

The following day the *Monarch of Bermuda* sailed down the Mersey and dropped anchor so that the other convoy ships could join us. I went on deck with my diary, leaned on the ship's rail and wrote:

Ten o'clock on a cold, blustery morning in Liverpool Bay. The sharp, yellow sunlight bathes the convoy of ships in a peculiar light so that they look unreal against the grey water. A plane circles round and makes a perfect landing on an aircraft-carrier. We are in the second ship of the convoy. In our wake sails a smaller vessel, so close that we can count the men on her decks. We shall set sail shortly for an unknown destination.

While we were carrying out our lifeboat drill on 15 February with the sea now aquamarine, now turquoise in brilliant sunshine, word spread that Winston Churchill was about to speak on the wireless. After the drill everyone trooped into the lounge-bars or amidships to hear broadcast the shocking news of the fall of Singapore to the Japanese. Now we knew we would not be sailing to Malaya as had been rumoured but to the Middle East or India.

The *Monarch of Bermuda*, which was to be our home for the next five weeks, was an outsize yacht of the Furness Withy line. She had been on the New York to Bermuda run for about ten years and her standards of comfort and adornment were excellent. She had been repainted when she was hurriedly transformed from a luxury liner into a troopship in 1939; as far as I remember, her superstructure was white, with the hull a pale grey. This sober colouring contrasted with the devil-may-care impression given by her three rakish funnels.

The spiral stairway leading to the dining saloon was wide and thickly carpeted. If you were late for a meal and had to hurry, you were liable to run into the arms of a young naval officer, which was quite a pleasant experience. A spacious plushy foyer led into the finely proportioned dining saloon,

Monarch of Bermuda, 1943.

whose furniture could be latched down to the floor in foul weather. But it was the architectural features which drew the eye. Everything was vaguely oriental, much use being made of coloured glass and hidden lighting, the central lantern window letting extra daylight through its stained-glass panels. The glazed, metal-grilled side windows looked across a strip of deck to the ocean. It was easy to see why the *Monarch of Bermuda* had been known as the 'millionaires' ship'.

17 February 1942

Awoke to a steady rise and fall as we approached Greenock. Stayed on deck in spite of the stiff breeze. Many people seasick already. Doris and I put our names down for Arabic and Spanish classes. If only we knew where we were going we could learn the language of the country. Talked to two young Coast Defence subalterns. They look like schoolboys.

Tonight I stood on deck and watched the strange phenomenon of phosphorescence. As the foam curled away from the bows, marine will-o'-the-wisps flashed and glowed among the fan-shaped waves. There were stars overhead and the silver sickle of the new moon – sparks and torches below in the water.

The sisters took it in turn to work in the sick bay but there were no other duties. The time we spent in the swimming pool helped to counteract the effects of the unaccustomed good food. A physical training sergeant-instructor conducted early morning exercises on deck for the sisters, but no matter how early we got up we were always sure of an audience of interested sailors, soldiers and airmen, who tactfully pretended to be gazing out to sea. Boxing bouts were arranged for the men, who used one side of the deck while the officers used the other. Volunteers gave talks to the troops on hygiene and diet in the tropics. But the most popular of all activities was the amateur concert party. Those who could offer such skills as acting, singing or performing on a musical instrument were gathered together by a middle-aged officer from the London stage, who drilled us 'darlings' until we were capable of satisfying a not-too-critical audience. There wasn't a great a deal of talent but there was plenty of enthusiasm and after a week of rehearsals we were ready for our three-night concert.

The long emotion-filled silence that followed the singing by a young Yorkshire lass of that nostalgic lyric 'Linden Lea' was broken by our director crooning 'At the Balalaika' from a popular West End theatre production of that name. He was a plump man who unconsciously swayed his well-padded hips as he sang – an action that produced a barrage of ribald suggestions from the troops, inadequately covered by the fierce applause of the more kindly disposed. Then it was the turn of two colleagues and myself to do a 'Three Little Sisters' act, which consisted of a coy verse each about the army, navy and air force interspersed with a little drill in which we did a right turn, marched three paces forward, turned, then marched three paces back again. It was felt by our director that this simple piece of military manoeuvring would delight the conscripts.

The first evening this exercise went off very well and got a reasonable amount of applause, but on the second night of the concert I accidentally turned to face my two partners who, of course, marched into me. The resultant mêlée brought down the house and for the remaining performance I was instructed to repeat the mistake that every recruit dreads making.

After a week or so at sea a certain amount of fraternising between the sisters and officers had begun to take place, though we kept to our own tables for meals. I soon discovered that it was necessary to decide which group of men I was going to associate with during the voyage. At first I went round with Coastal Defence in the morning and Heavy Artillery in the evening but before long there was pressure put on me to make up my mind where I belonged. When I realised that there would be bad feeling between the groups if I didn't come to a decision, I tossed a coin. The Heavy Artillery won.

The subalterns of 340 Battery, 96 Heavy Anti-Aircraft Regiment, Royal Artillery – Dick Burton, Eric Pearce, 'Mitch' Mitchener and 'Charles the Schoolmaster' – soon introduced me to Captains Paddy Rowan, Geoffrey Mundell and Gerry Marlsdale. The young officers quickly 'roped' me in to give talks to their men on such subjects as Life in India, more for entertainment value than for educational content. I warned them that it would take a few days for me to prepare a lecture. What I didn't tell them was that I had never given a talk of any sort in public in my life. There were no appropriate books on board and the only ones I remembered reading on India were Kipling's *Just So Stories* and *The Jungle Book*, and E M Forster's *A Passage to India*.

Resting on my bunk in the afternoon, I allowed my mind to weave a background tapestry for the lecture with the shreds and strands of memories which formed a ravelled knot of associations conjured up by the word 'India'. The scarlet thread of glamour and romance that ran through the *Indian Love Lyrics* would make an introduction. I had discovered this popular book of songs by Amy Woodford-Findon among my mother's music when I was learning to play the piano at the age of twelve: 'Till I Wake', 'Less than the Dust', 'Temple Bells' and one that I could not remember. They suggested an exotic world peopled with princes from the Arabian Nights in jewelled turbans, riding on elephants hung with priceless Kashmir rugs; and sari-clad ladies, with gems in their nostrils, feeding rose petals and sherbet to snow-white does.

Another strand of memory took me back again to my childhood, when a picture in the *Lancashire Daily Post* caught my eye. An emaciated little Indian in spectacles, dressed in a white sheet, stood in the centre of a group of cotton workers – chiefly women – outside a mill at Darwen. He had been explaining to them why it was so necessary for India to finish and process her own cotton, thus depriving Lancashire of its livelihood. The listeners evidently felt the force of his arguments for they appeared to be quite friendly towards him. The little man was Mahatma Gandhi, who had been representing the Congress Party of India at the Round Table Conference in London in 1931. We would be hearing a great deal more about Gandhi when we reached India, I thought; in fact our very lives might depend on his attitude to Indian Independence. I must certainly mention him.

Giving the talk on India was rather more alarming than I had anticipated. The troops, on their best behaviour, sat in rows with their sergeant-major very much in evidence and the subalterns lurking in the background. I was never asked to lecture again, which was a relief to me as well as to my captive audience no doubt. All the same, it gave the men something to talk about and helped me to get over my shyness in the matter of speaking in public.

27 February 1942

The weather grows hotter every day. The sea-water baths we take each evening (fresh water is rationed) leave us feeling sticky and salty. It is in the cabins at night that the heat becomes really oppressive, despite the electric fans. The swimming-bath opened today. Luckily Doris and I had packed our bathing costumes so we shall swim each morning before breakfast. We all drank something called a 'Horse's Neck' to counteract the commanding officer's pungent speech. He fears that everyone is becoming indolent and dissipated but I think the possibility of a sudden emergency is at the back of everybody's mind.

'My' battery introduced me to their major, Maurice Hobbiss; red-haired, avuncular, friendly. The men obviously liked and trusted him. I also met their colonel, Kenneth Hargreaves[1] from Yorkshire, fortyish and a bachelor. He was a shy man with the ladies like many professional soldiers, broad in the shoulders and tall, with a leonine head, very blue eyes and strong white teeth which made me think of the wolf in Red Riding Hood. Yet he was not a 'wolf' by nature; conventional and public-spirited I imagined.

One fortunate group of officers had a tame comedian to keep them amused. We came upon them in a quiet corner of the deck, bent double in an effort to suppress their laughter. In the centre of the huddle was a tall man doing a brilliant imitation of a senior staff officer on board, a hard-bitten, much-wounded First World War VC whose name was Carton de Wiart. The comedian's name was le Mesurier. Many years later I thought that he must have been that splendid, well-loved actor John le Mesurier of 'Dad's Army' fame who died in 1983. Whoever the officer was, he most certainly had a gift for mimicry.

Major-General Carton de Wiart cannot have been far off retirement, though his disabilities from the Great War probably put a few years on to his age. He wore a black patch over one eye, had an arm immobilised and walked with a pronounced limp so that he looked every inch a war hero. His VC had been gained at La Boiselle near Albert in 1916, when he was serving with the 8th Battalion, The Gloucestershire Regiment. The young men admired his exploits and he was frequently a topic of conversation in the bar.

The *Awatea*, a New Zealand vessel, sailed astern; sometimes she was plainly visible, sometimes absent for days on end. There must have been some twenty ships in the convoy, not counting

1 Later Brigadier Kenneth Hargreaves. Lord-Lieutenant of West Yorkshire, 1974–1978.

HMS *Formidable* at sea, 1943.

the escorts. We often noticed planes landing on the aircraft-
carrier and watched a fast-moving destroyer weaving in and
out among the transports. There were stories going round that
the previous convoy, bound for Malaya, had been bombed with
great loss of life but we didn't really believe them, any more
than we believed the constant rumours of misbehaviour on the
ship spread about by wishful thinkers. We suspected the cabin
stewards of being the purveyors of these provocative insinuations, the key word being 'purveyors' in the exact dictionary
sense of 'suppliers of something needed'. A thousand men and
sixty women meant a lack of female company for large numbers of men, who in their deprivation might feel that a little
titillating excitement was better than nothing at all, particularly
as there was such a dearth of occupations for the mind. One
story averred that a pink brassière had blown in through the
galley porthole and fallen into the brown Windsor soup that
the cook was dishing up; another, that under the canvas-
covered lifeboats on the boat deck at night there flourished
unimaginable debauchery; well, not 'unimaginable' perhaps,
because it was the ability to imagine such impropriety that made
it all worthwhile.

With the issue of bolsters in the very hot weather a *frisson*
of excitement shot round the ship. When Doris and I came
down to our cabin one day we found an extra pillow on the
bunks. The cabin steward said that they were 'Dutch husbands',
leaving us none the wiser. However we tucked them under our

knees at night like the 'donkeys' we used in hospital to keep the patients from sliding down the bed, and found that they kept us cooler. These bolsters were a source of burgeoning innuendo, but the subalterns of 'my' battery would have no more countenanced such suggestive talk than they would have used foul language in front of me.

Later on my 'army square' veil disappeared from the cabin. After many fruitless inquiries I traced the 'theft' to one of the young naval officers who – it was alleged – slept with it under his pillow. This was a delicate situation. I didn't want to deprive the young man of his romantic imaginings, but I only possessed two veils and I couldn't wear the same one all the way to our final destination. After a searching conversation with the cabin steward, whom I suspected of being involved, the white organdie square appeared again on my bunk – all beautifully laundered.

We were given permission to change into tropical kit on 28 February as we were sailing round the bulge of Africa. Thereafter the naval officers certainly had the edge on the other services. As they stood on deck in their snow-white shirts and drill shorts with spotless white knee socks and shoes, they made the khaki-clad army and air force officers look very drab, particularly as their so-called 'shorts' were down past their knees and baggy with it. There were volunteers among the sisters who were willing to do a bit of hand-sewing for those whose shorts were too droopy. Those sisters who had mufti dresses or tennis shorts were allowed to wear them, the rest wore the white drill frock with scarlet and white epaulettes which was the tropical uniform of the QAs. The dresses were rather impractical as they had a dozen round pearl buttons down the front which had to be taken out and reslotted into each fresh dress. The buttons were kept in place with metal pins and it took quite a long time to change into a clean frock. Once we reached India this aggravating task was undertaken by servants.

On 3 March we had our first sight of Africa, our ship anchoring alone outside Freetown, Sierra Leone, early in the morning. We opened our porthole excitedly to breathe in the African air, astonished at how clearly defined everything looked. Does anyone ever forget their first sight of a foreign land? My diary says:

The Dark Continent at last. Quite different from anything I had imagined. It is green and hilly and the colours are so vivid that it reminds me of a Technicolor film. The young men and boys come out to the ship in frail boats made out of hollowed-out trees which they handle with great skill. They shout for pennies and 'Glasgow tanners' which they dive for, behaving like dolphins, turning and twisting in the clear water and never missing a coin. A boat came out with the mail and no one left the ship and the following day we set sail once more, grateful for the slight breeze in the tropical heat.

Day after day the gunners practised their artillery drill and one heard snatches of conversation about 'drift' and other mysterious technical effects. During a dance on deck for the officers and sisters we watched a total eclipse of the moon and saw shooting stars streak across the heavens. Then it was the turn of the troops to relax and arrangements were made for an afternoon of dancing. The soldiers and airmen were instructed by their officers (who were not allowed to join in on this occasion) to place a clean folded handkerchief in their left hands so that their sweating palms should not sully the white uniforms of the sisters. It struck me as odd that hands should sweat if one were in the ranks but not if one had a commission!

The best dancers in the forces were the sergeants and corporals who had spent their Saturday nights at the local Palais de Danse in civilian life. I found this to apply wherever I went in India. It was the one activity that gave them the chance to outshine the officers and they were well aware of it.

16 March 1942

Captain Paddy Rowan's birthday party. We all enjoyed ourselves. Colonel Ken in good form. Introduced to handsome Geoffrey Lavers, the assistant adjutant, who has made a vow not to dance with anyone until he returns home to his wife. Subalterns and I very impressed. Talked to Charles, the schoolmaster, about poetry. Charles is very thin and dark, tall and slightly stooping. He says he was in India when a child but doesn't remember much about it. He's the quietest of the four, self-effacing, serious but whimsical; probably the most mature. Dick is a nice ordinary chap, predictable and ideal for a shipboard friendship – after all no one wants to get involved emotionally at this stage of the war. Eric attracts me more

– he's a great reader – but he is spoken for. Mitch is beautiful; calm, thoughtful and detached. I think he is newly-wed so must be feeling miserable. It's like having four spendid brothers. Geoffrey and Paddy are sweet, but in the next generation. As for Gerry Marlsdale, well, we all call him 'Auntie Maud' because he fusses over us.

The young officers were acutely aware of the difference in living standards between themselves and their men. I imagine the situation was not all that different from that which existed in troopships in the First World War with crowded rough conditions for the ranks and superior accommodation for the officers. I had seen the soldiers' quarters in the bowels of the ship, which were not at all salubrious, with hammocks or bunks in cramped spaces and bare wooden tables to eat off. The backgrounds of men and officers were often identical – schoolmasters, bank clerks, business reps – and this brought home to both the incongruities of the system. Still, old habits die hard. Though now and again private soldiers would ascend to the higher deck to look longingly through the large windows at the elegantly served food in the dining saloon and the subalterns would mutter angrily about the unfair treatment of the ranks, nothing was ever changed.

We were ordered to carry our life-jackets around with us at all times, their bulky, kapok-filled pillows proving to be more of a nuisance than the neat boxed gasmasks we had toted about at home. As a result, they were constantly being left behind in the bar or on deck, their owners flying into a panic when bells rang for an emergency lifeboat drill, which the captain laid on occasionally to keep us on our toes.

For the regular practice once a week we assembled at our stations in rows of a dozen people, each with a senior officer in charge, who rounded up the dilatory ones. The lifeboats were winched down to sea level and sometimes a few sailors would go for a row to show us how safe they were. I remember standing there for an hour at a time with the sun on my face and a stiff breeze whipping my hair backwards, feeling exceedingly bored, while our leader passed along the line checking that our life-jackets were securely tied to prevent them floating up and throttling us in the sea during a real emergency.

I listened to the men in our row talking and began to realise how vulnerable to a determined attack a troopship could be: one well-placed bomb or torpedo and we would be putting our lifeboat drill into action. The presence of our escorting warships was reassuring. The activities on HMS *Formidable*, the great bare-decked carrier which was seldom out of sight, never lost their fascination for me and many of the other passengers. Planes came and went with great assurance and panache, skidding to a standstill like swans on a lake when you thought they had no hope of pulling up in time. We lined the ship's rail daily to marvel at the display.

One sunlit afternoon I followed with my eye a solitary fighter as it swept close to the water, its butterfly shadow changing the pale blue of the ocean to aquamarine. As it neared the carrier it undershot the deck, tipped sideways and plunged beneath the waves.

This event shocked us all into silence. The cold certainty that there were no survivors prevented us from discussing it. Violent death at sea was something we had not come to terms with. I did not record the event in my diary, finding it impossible to jot down such a tragedy among the daily trivia yet not feeling equal to describing it in detail along with the high-flown accounts of natural phenomena. The weather changed in conformity with our mood:

> The temperature has dropped this morning; the ocean looks dangerous and brooding. We are rolling heavily in a sea as grey and viscous as molten lava. The water in the ship's wake changes to a vivid shade of 'eau de nil' as the air whips through it. The wind is rising, shrieking through the boat-deck and howling sonorously in the funnels. The ship lurches and shudders as the swell increases. It starts to rain – a fine, misty drizzle that wraps us in obscurity. Standing at the ship's rail I can only see the nearest waves, now bottle-green and glassy.

A great many people became seasick, even the good sailors finding it difficult to keep their balance when moving along the companionways. The dining saloon attendance was halved and the cabin stewards were kept busy. During dinner one day there was a sudden squall and the sound of smashed crockery. The chair I was occupying slid across the room, depositing me in the purser's lap to our mutual embarrassment. Mr Pushie was a dour Scot, getting on in years, with the reputation of being a misogynist. He ordered the stewards to fasten the chairs to the floor, continuing his meal as though nothing had happened;

On the boat deck of a troopship during the Second World War.

but he always gave me a half-civil nod when I passed his solitary table afterwards.

Well brought up young women were expected to be exceedingly proper in those days and perhaps my convent education made me more proper than most. It was the custom to parade round the deck in groups at dusk on the darkened ship, unless you happened to be a bar addict or a bridge player. Sometimes a couple detached themselves from the main group and drifted towards the rail to admire the phosphorescence or the night sky; thus I found myself one evening in the company of a pleasant young subaltern from 'my' battery. We enjoyed our conversation so much that it was 11pm before we parted. It was all so innocent – just the pressure of a hand and a goodnight kiss on the cheek – but the following morning the other lieutenants teased me, one of them drawing me aside to ask me if I was aware that my companion of the previous night was married. I was struck dumb with mortification for a moment, blushed furiously, then asked him angrily why they

55

had not told me before as I would certainly not have walked round the deck alone with a married man. This story quickly got back to the colonel of the regiment, Kenneth Hargreaves, who was so impressed that he decided that I should be made Honorary Colonel of the battery.

Because Fort St George had been the first port of call for the *Monarch* during her peacetime cruises to Hamilton in Bermuda, St George's Day had always been celebrated on board. Our thoughtful captain, who said he could not possibly allow his passengers to leave his ship at Durban without experiencing the delights and extravagances of that patronal festival, exercised his pastoral powers and proclaimed St George's Day to be a moveable feast, solemnised this year on Friday 20 March.

There was a short service in the morning followed by twelve hours of entertainment. I was wined and dined at Major Hobbiss's table, after which 340 Battery was duly dubbed 'Angela's Own'. Colonel Ken gallantly wrote on my menu 'Thanks for your good influence on "Angela's Own"' and all the other officers signed the menu with suitable (gentlemanly) comments. It was a splendid evening, closing with a toast to the patron saint drunk in Nuits-St-Georges. We who in England had been subject to severe rationing, carrying our little tins of butter and sugar around with us, were still unused to the abundant food supplies of high quality and great variety provided throughout the voyage.

Despite the late party, most of us were up on deck by 8am next morning for our first sight of Durban, gazing out across the unbelievably blue water to the dazzling assortment of small vessels clustered together in a marina to the left of the harbour. Dick Burton, Geoffrey Mundell and I were given shore leave, crossing to the palm-lined beach in a crowded launch, grateful for the breeze on what was to be the hottest day of our stay.

Seated in a café an hour later I took out my diary and wrote:

Durban is a most beautiful city whose groves of trees and tall white buildings are silhouetted against the green hills beyond. The elegant houses have wide verandahs, cool informal gardens and brilliant flowering trees. At last we can examine our first palm trees and watch the lovely little brown children playing in their shade. We were astonished to see warriors with elaborate feathered head-dresses waiting beside their hand-drawn rickshaws. They looked

MENU

FURNESS-BERMUDA LINE

Menu.

Fillets of Anchovy on Toast

Cream St. George

River Dee Salmon, Parsley Sauce

Baked York Ham, Cumberland Sauce
Roast Surrey Capon, Bread Sauce

Prime Ribs and Sirloin of Beef, Yorkshire Pudding
Fresh Garden Peas
Boiled and Browned Potatoes

English Plum Pudding, Brandy Sauce
Assorted Pastry

Cheese and Crackers

Dessert   Coffee

I travell'd among unknown men
In lands beyond the sea;
Nor, England! did I know till then
What love I bore to thee.

W. Wordsworth.

Menu for the St George's Day dinner aboard the *Monarch of Bermuda*,
20 March 1942.

too magnificent for such a humble service.

Durban appears to be a popular seaside resort for Europeans. There are not many Africans about. The waiters are Indians as are many of the shopkeepers. Everything looks so clean, fresh and smoke-free compared with England. How fortunate that General Smuts sided with the Allies in this war. If the Germans were in control here, how would we have reached India?

What a luxury it was to be able to buy unlimited supplies of soap, powder and lipstick in the well-stocked shops; to enter shoe and handbag stores where there were several styles of white sandals on offer; and to choose wide bands of black and brown velvet ribbon to make up into bows for those of us with long back hair – it being *de rigeur* for the front hair to be swept upwards on top of the head.

Along the esplanade, several expensive-looking cars were parked, their well-groomed owners standing beside them. They greeted us with smiles and welcoming handshakes. These were representatives of English firms in Durban waiting to meet uniformed colleagues from home in order to give them a taste of South African hospitality. Many of the Afrikaner residents, too, went out of their way to offer the servicemen lifts and invite them to their homes for meals.

Geoffrey, Dick and I went to see the film *Bitter Sweet*, following it up with a dinner dance at the Marine Hotel where the band played 'I'll See You Again' by popular request as we waltzed on a real dance floor instead of a wooden deck. There we were joined by Eric Pearce, Mitch and a QA sister called Helen, who insisted on accompanying us on an exhilarating rickshaw ride back to the harbour. We sat out on the deck of the *Empire Pride*, the ship to which 340 Battery were moving for the rest of the voyage, and talked until two o'clock in the morning. Nobody wanted to go to bed, what with the excitement of being in South Africa, experiencing so many new sights and sounds and contemplating the brilliance of the necklace of harbour lights against the velvety darkness.

The next day was spent in transferring ourselves and our baggage into the India-bound ships while others in the convoy prepared to sail for Egypt. Doris, the McKenzies and I found ourselves on the *Stratheden*, which we thought very inferior to the *Monarch*. 340 Battery dubbed their ship the *Altmark* after the German prison ship of that name.

Durban harbour, 1941.

As there were only two days left before we sailed everyone that could be spared was given shore leave. I accompanied Dick Burton, who came from Norwich, to the Durban office of the assurance firm he worked for at home, where we met Billy, his opposite number, who insisted on showing us the sights. Eric, Mitch, Geoffrey and two QAs joined us for drinks at a place called the Roadhouse. Then we moved on to the Edward Hotel, a palatial establishment which made the Adelphi Hotel in Liverpool seem like a poor relation. The Singapore gin slings served there, ornamented with the most exotic fruits, were a joy to the eye and the palate, proving to be almost a meal in themselves on a hot day. This was our first experience of the innate dignity of the soft-footed, elegantly attired Indian servants, with their neat turbans and cummerbunds, on whose unobtrusive service so many Europeans depended for a bearable life out East. The war news culled from a newspaper was that the Japanese were in Burma, having entered via Siam and French Indo-China; there was silence from Singapore. One of the men got out a map to show me how near Burma was to

India but his concern made very little impact on me. It was hard to imagine fighting going on in beautiful tropical places such as Singapore. I finished my gin sling and pushed all thought of the war out of my head; there would be time enough when it was on our doorstep.

On our final day Billy took Helen, Eric, Dick and me out to the country behind Durban where we had lunch at a restaurant in the wilds. The fruit we saw astounded us; it was so large and luscious, particularly the grapes. The sun was hot but not unbearably so; there was a freshness in the air that would no doubt disappear with the tropical summer of the southern hemisphere. Many service people declared that they would return to settle down in South Africa after the war for it appeared to be a veritable Garden of Eden.

That evening a party of thirteen of us went to the Edward Hotel for dinner, then danced at the Roadhouse until midnight, after which we said goodbye to Billy, who had put his huge low-slung car at our disposal and acted as chauffeur throughout our stay. In the morning we embarked on the *Stratheden*.

A few days out from Durban, the destroyer HMS *Panther* came to pay a social call, making it possible for us to catch up on our strictly censored news of the convoy. We told the crew how safe it made us feel to see the *Panther* zig-zagging along the horizon like a sheep dog taking care of its flock. Looking down on those naval officers and ratings from the top deck of the *Stratheden* I suddenly felt a lump in my throat, and a surge of patriotism swept over me for the first time during the voyage. They looked so vulnerable in their small ship on the immense expanse of the Indian Ocean devotedly guarding their fellow countrymen.

The nine other ships in the convoy disappeared from view at intervals, filling me with consternation. The first time this happened I thought the *Empire Pride* had gone for ever. On Colonel Ken's advice I adopted another of his batteries – 293 – but I was half-hearted about my role for I missed the beautiful *Monarch* and all my old companions. I was glad to be given some sick bay duties in the afternoon and quickly grew some- what introspective, using my diary as a sounding board:

26 March 1942

Sometimes I feel like two people. I am the young woman enjoying the relationships with strange, interesting human beings, feeling exhilarated to think that any moment I could meet someone very special indeed. This part of me is frivolous and self-centred at times; sad and depressed at others. Then there is another person in me, deeper and more self-contained, always at peace, who feels at home in contemplating the elements, the fathomless ocean, the eternal stars; for whom music and poetry express all the feelings that cannot be put into words because they are too tremendous. Does everyone feel like this I wonder – except that people are inspired by different things, like painting – or perhaps even cricket or football! Is the difference just one of degree? I wish Charles were here. He might know the answer.

In the bar one evening someone pointed out a plumpish, dark-haired man with a small moustache as Ross Parker, composer of 'There'll always be an England'. Even at that time it was considered that his song would be to the Second World War what 'Pack up your Troubles' had been to the Great War. I noticed that he found the heat trying; the strength of the sun in the Indian Ocean took everyone by surprise. Only the most dedicated continued to play deck tennis; the rest crowded into deck-chairs in the shade or lounged in the cool bar, listlessly stirring ice into a gin and lemon drink called a Tom Collins. The sea became so smooth that one expected it to wrinkle like the surface of cream rather than break up into waves.

29 March, Palm Sunday

We have now entered upon the most magical part of our voyage. Terrifically hot day with lightning flashing continually. The Indian Ocean is calm as a mirror; the water so clear that one can see far down into the depths and watch the marine life. Porpoises sport in the distance under a huge golden moon. Shoals of flying-fish accompany us like a flock of iridescent birds, dipping and rising alongside. Drowsy thoughts of what it would be like to be becalmed on the glassy ocean like the ship in 'The Ancient Mariner' drift through one's brain in the noonday heat.

During the last week of the voyage there were more couples walking the deck than ever before. Even the wallflowers found partners because nobody wanted to waste the rare combination of warmth, beauty and tropical glamour. On 2 April a celebration was held to mark the end of what had seemed like a seven-week holiday cruise, despite the continuing possibility of enemy attack. Colonel Ken gave a party in his cabin when I tasted Drambuie for the first time, finding it very sweet and strong – in fact it took my breath away.

Afterwards there was a dance on deck with a genuine instrumental band. Baby-faced Second Lieutenant Dick Amsden of 96 Field Company, RA, who looked much too young to go to war, was too shy to dance but asked if he might write to me when we went our separate ways. Gordon Brock of 293 Battery, a tall lieutenant with a completely bald head even though he was still in his twenties, was an excellent dancer, as was the Scotsman, Captain Charlie Brown from 405 Searchlight Battery. I saved the last waltz for Colonel Ken (who had thoughtfully changed into his white tennis shoes for the dancing), appreciative of the fact that he had kept an avuncular eye on me during the voyage. By the end of the evening I realised that I had promised to write to eight men from the two ships so long as they wrote to me first. I hoped I would be able to keep it up.

Doris and I agreed to stay together if we could when we reached India. The two McKenzie girls also planned to ask for the same postings. These two could not have been more different in nature or appearance: Isobel, oval-faced with a milk and roses complexion and dark-blue tilted eyes, had a serene attitude to life; Dora was small, brisk and practical. I could well imagine her as a district nurse in Scotland after the war. I came across Isobel several times in India but she eventually developed a chest complaint which required treatment in South Africa. I never saw Dora again.

On Easter Day there was an open air service conducted by the captain. Looking round the deck of the *Stratheden* I thought that everyone appeared to be rather subdued now that we were to be faced with the reality of war in a country of intense heat and primitive conditions where we would be scattered like a handful of corn over the vast subcontinent. England seemed a world away; I wondered if the bombs were still falling and if my family was safe. I felt rather depressed, fearing that the war might go on for a long time.

In the early hours of 8 April we were awakened by the vibrating rattle of a running chain and the hooting of many sirens. The *Stratheden* had crept through an archipelago of little islands during the night to present us with a dawn view of a palm-fringed shore with the mountains of the Western Ghats beyond. To the left the great commercial and municipal buildings that make Bombay one of the most memorable cities in the world stood etched against the skyline by the risen sun.

Sitting on deck sorting out the contents of my shoulder bag while I waited to leave the ship, I came across the last letter I had received from my sister Barbara just before we embarked at Liverpool docks. Peter Horsman, a family friend the same age as myself, had been killed in an accident in the forces. Hugo Kolb, who had taken me out in the second year of the war to celebrate becoming a pilot officer in the RAF, was a prisoner in Java, having been captured by the Japanese before Singapore fell. When I looked up I noticed that the *Empire Pride* was back alongside. It would be pleasant to see my friends who were aboard her once more. I took out my diary to make the last entry of the voyage: 'Well, here I am abroad at last,' I wrote, 'which is what I wanted, so I had better make the most of it. India, here I come!'

It took several hours to clear the ship but at last we stood upon terra firma looking about us in dazed wonder. Porters with identifying numbers on their shabby red cotton uniforms fought each other for the privilege of carrying our luggage. As they trotted along to the waiting taxis, balancing the heavy trunks on their turban-protected heads, their spindly legs seemed to bend into a bow shape with the weight of their burdens.

A group of us from the *Stratheden* met at the Taj Mahal Hotel, where we stayed for dinner because the restaurant was air-conditioned and we could not bear the unaccustomed heat outside. Afterwards we came back to the ship to sleep on board for the last time.

The following day everybody sent airgraphs home to say that they were in India. I said goodbye to Colonel Ken and the rest of the regiment, then spent the remainder of the day with 'Angela's Own', comparing notes on our respective shipboard experiences. At 7pm Doris and I joined twenty-six other sisters at the railway station where we all had to identify and claim our luggage. Hundreds of desperately poor ragged families thronged the platforms, looking for unoccupied spaces to sleep in, which made it impossible to reach the train without stepping over recumbent bodies. There were four of us to a compartment with a bunk for each sister and a minute washroom.

Shutters with tiny perforations covered the windows to keep out dust and thieves, the latter being quite capable of crawling along the train roof and thrusting their hands into the compartment to steal cases, we were told. The noise on the platform was ear-splitting after the quietness of the ship. Vendors of tea and soft drinks shouted their wares, guards argued with would-be passengers and porters called to each other as they loaded our piles of luggage into the end compartments. Beggars hawked and spat red spittle, which made me think that they must be in an advanced state of tuberculosis. There was an all-pervading spicey, pungent smell that one could only describe as 'Essence of India'.

Shortly after 7.30pm the immensely long train moved slowly out of the Victoria railway terminus, with its curious array of towers and battlements, for a two-night journey across the centre of India to Howrah station, Calcutta. As night fell with a swift obliteration of the scenery, we took turns in standing under the thin trickle of the shower in the washroom.

We all slept badly. With the filtering of the first light through the metal grilles, I slid down from the top bunk to let a little air into the stuffy compartment. The freshness of the morning filled my grateful lungs. Caught by the early beams of a pale sunrise, our train was rounding a bend, its hinderpart of twenty coaches snaking through the desolate prospect. As the day progressed we were torn between sitting in the dark with the shutters down to keep out the dust and sun, or opening them so that we could watch the passing landscape. The flat Deccan plain stretched to the horizon, bereft of any undulations to break the monotony. Wherever the white Indian bullocks wandered on the herbage beside a stagnant pool, yellow-billed egrets could be seen dabbling in the greenery for grasshoppers or catching flies on the backs of the cattle. Patient, wide-horned water-buffaloes wallowed in the mud up to the nostrils.

We were charmed with the beauty of the children who clamoured for alms at every station along the route but distressed by their manifest hunger and poverty. We had little to give them. Our food was handed in at the door by white-clad bearers, whose cummerbunds and turbans bore the insignia of the railway they served. As we approached Nagpur, the half-way station, a magnificent bird, kingfisher-blue, flashed across the line, while small monkeys perched in the palm trees at the station's approach chattered noisily.

At Nagpur our diet was supplemented with oranges which

Victoria Railway Terminus, Bombay, 1944.

we bought from vendors on the platform, oranges which had a completely different flavour from those we used to buy in England before the war. Nagpur, we heard from a friendly Indian clerk who poked his head in at the door, was the chief orange-growing area of India. He warned us about buying the fruit from hawkers as, he said, the men injected them with water to make them plumper and the water might be infected. His advice came too late: we had all eaten them. As it turned out, none of us was any the worse for the experience.

Besides Doris, Mary McNally and Jean Hamilton shared the compartment. We continued to take turns under the shower during the hottest part of the day, lying on the bunks in our underwear most of the time wondering aloud how we could cope with the climate. As we neared Calcutta we saw signs of civilisation – the gardens of isolated jute managers' houses – where I thought I recognised scarlet poinsettias and hibiscus flowers, though I had only seen them in pictures.

The train steamed into Howrah station at 11am on the second morning. We expected it to be cooler when we left the crowded

65

platforms to climb into the ambulances, marked with a red cross, that carried us from the station precincts across Howrah Bridge to the British military hospital. But it was a case of out of the frying-pan into the fire: the moist heat was truly awful – and it was still only April. During our journey throngs of Indians blocked the narrow streets, frequently slowing us down to a standstill.

Matron greeted us with the news that we were not expected for another week, giving orders for our luggage to be taken to a large tent, where we put up our camp beds, canvas wash-basins and low canvas baths with matching buckets. Those who had taken camping holidays before the war found themselves in great demand as we struggled to make ends of wood and canvas meet. Eventually we fathomed what a piece of equipment called a tent-pole strap was for; it was to tie round the central pole of the tent in order that we should have somewhere to hang up our clothes. For the first time we laid out our lined canvas bedding-rolls, which contained a rough blanket and canvas pillow cover, arranging them on our camp beds with the blanket stuffed inside to make a pillow. A dhobi arrived to take away the uniforms we had used on the journey, returning them on hangers in starched splendour within twenty-four hours.

After a few days Doris and I were offered a room in the much-coveted living quarters at the rather overcrowded No. 5 Minto Park, in a pleasant tree-lined road near the hospital. We now had a solid roof over our heads but still needed to use our camping equipment. To celebrate our first free day we took rickshaws to the centre of Calcutta, visiting the officers' club for a swim in the pool to escape the heat, then sampling the cinema in the evening. The 'Picture Palace' was curiously primitive for such a cosmopolitan city – rather like a village hall in England but with creaking punkahs whirling overhead and the added risk of being savaged by the bugs that dwelt in their thousands in the wickerwork chairs. We were told by Tony Ridler, an RAF flight lieutenant who got into conversation with us when the Claudette Colbert film broke down for the second time, that even the first-class hotels were not immune from bed-bug infestation and – something much worse – occasional outbreaks of cholera.

It came as a shock to me to notice the easy assumption of superiority over the Indians by the British residents in Calcutta. It wasn't that they were overbearing or insulting towards the servants and clerks – more as though the Indians were part of the décor, not really human beings at all. I was reminded of the behaviour of some of the sisters towards the probationers in my training days. Service people newly out from the United Kingdom, after an initial interest in Indians as individuals, adopted the prevalent attitude of indifference. I am speaking of the day-to-day commerce of a big city; in the service cantonments things were probably conducted in a more humane and personal manner.

Two days after arriving in Calcutta I found myself on the officers' ward of the very well-organised peacetime hospital. Several of the doctors were Austrian-Jewish psychoanalysts, who had escaped before Hitler annexed Austria. Our patients were mainly victims of malarial and dysentery-type illnesses, plus a few wounded members of the indigenous Frontier Force Rifles, a regiment with unrivalled knowledge and experience of tribal warfare on the North West Frontier. I was put in charge of one of their officers, a Major Hugh Sealy of the 4th Battalion, who was suffering from a severe head wound. Twice he nearly died but finally recovered enough to be sent off to convalesce at the military hospital at Poona. Because we considered him to be a little at risk after such a severe injury we asked him to keep in touch with us for several months. Major Sealy was just one of the hundreds of casualties, many of them suffering from starvation and exhaustion in the retreat from Burma, that were filling our hospital beds. It took several weeks for us to understand what was happening as the newspapers gave nothing away and service personnel knew better than to ask questions, having been imbued with the axiom that 'Careless talk costs lives'.

We were soon introduced to the mysteries of Indian cooking. As I came off duty one afternoon, I peeped into the cookhouse of the sisters' mess out of idle curiosity. The old *khansama* (cook) was working alone in what appeared to be chaos and the odour of charred chicken pervaded the air. He was so dried up and brown and his garments so redolent of cooking *ghee* that he looked and smelled like one of his own culinary failures. All of us depended on the *khansama*'s expertise on his charcoal stove for our legs of chicken (miniscule Indian chickens), curries and stewed lamb – or was it goat? Rice was served with everything, though we were allowed a few potatoes now and then. Vegetable dishes were disappointing. There were slithery, green ladies' fingers, purple aubergines and several varieties of pulses. Such puddings as there were tended to be ones introduced to

Opposite and above: members of 96 HAA Regiment, Royal Artillery, at Barrackpore, 1942. Top left: left to right, 'Charles the Schoolmaster', Maurice Hobbiss, Paddy Rowan and Geoffrey Mundell. Bottom left: Eric Pearce (left) and Dick Burton. Above: left to right, 'Mitch' Mitchener, Eric Pearce and Dick Burton.

India by British memsahibs – caramel custard, ground rice and cabinet pudding – while the excellent seasonal fruits such as mangoes, bananas, pineapples and custard-apples provided a welcome alternative in the hot weather.

Realising that most of the clothes we had brought with us were totally unsuited to India, we packed away in our steel trunks all our cold climate uniform – grey brimmed hats with scarlet bands and badges; heavy grey winter coats trimmed with scarlet round the collar, suitable for the North Pole; and really well-designed barathea suits, double-breasted and belted, with scarlet edging to collar and revers which had been made to measure by Shirley Smith, the tailors. We had worn them in Oxford with white poplin blouses and silver-grey ties, their smartness encouraging us to invest in black silk stockings and expensive black lace-up shoes to enhance the effect. The schoolgirl hats had been a drawback and we had left them off when we attended a dance or visited a restaurant. When there was a shortage of materials later in the war, all the services connected with the army went into khaki and our lovely suits of scarlet and grey were never worn again.

On 16 April Doris heard that 340 Battery and the rest of the RAs were in town, or rather that they were stationed at a reinforcement camp a few miles out of Calcutta. For the next twelve days we were able to meet quite frequently, making the most of our time before our permanent postings. We did the rounds of the Saturday Club, the Grand, Firpo's and Prince's Restaurant, while some of the men visited a night club, a shady dive called the Porto Rico where they were well and truly fleeced. At the Lighthouse cinema *Birth of the Blues* was showing erratically. Every day the swimming pool was lined with dozens of half-baked sunbathers hoping to achieve a tan before the hot weather started in earnest, making sunbathing impossible.

On 27 April Sisters Waller and Wyber accompanied me to the Calcutta bazaar. I wrote:

I tried to disentangle the odours that assailed my nostrils as I entered the Aladdin's Cave of curiosities: cow dung from the fires, spices from the stall near the entrance, horse urine from the passing *gharies* and an all-pervading coconut smell from the barber's stall, which took me back to my aunt's shack on Formby shore. The ripe fruit brings its own gallimaufrey of scents, attracting flies in their hundreds. The poor babies' eyes are covered in flies too and their pathetic pot-bellied bodies are wasted and shrivelled. By observation we discovered that the brick-red spittle on the pavements was the result of the native habit of chewing *pan*, a mixture of areca nut and betel leaf.

We noticed a terribly disabled man without fingers shuffling around on a little cart, begging for backsheesh. Is he a leper, I wonder? There are so many poor people wandering about who look as if they never have enough to eat. No one takes any notice! Little boys offered to carry our purchases in baskets on their heads, first twisting a grey rag of padding turban-wise to protect themselves. They all swarmed around shouting for attention until a smart, khaki-clad Indian policeman raised his baton to chase them away. It is quite alarming to see the desperate need for a few annas.

The stall-holders in their clean white *dhotis* look fairly prosperous. Many of the young men own a bicycle, which they share with a friend, one of them sitting on the handlebars. Other young men go about in pairs holding hands, reminding me of the way young English girls walk about arm-in-arm at a certain age to give themselves courage in facing the world – and in particular the young men in it. The bicycle bells ring all the time as their owners try to break through the solid phalanx of overloaded buses and Jehu-driven taxis.

When we went into a bank to change some money there was a white cow lying by the counter chewing its cud. No one attempted to drive it out. It was rather lovely with a hump on its back, the eyes as liquidly dark as a Jersey cow's. What a contrast the great granite buildings make with the dusty excremental street outside, where the heat blasts you with its foetid breath. Beggars accosted us all the way back to the Grand Hotel where we were rescued by the rickshaw wallahs, who drove us home.

When we returned to the hospital we saw a list of names on the notice-board. Six sisters were to be posted to Asansol, Bengal, and I was one of them.

Once more I started to pack my steel trunk, checking the list in my diary: thermometer, forceps, Wellington boots, tea-infuser, tin kettle, Beatrice stove, folding lantern. They were present and correct except for the lantern which had been unobtainable in England. Then the enamel plate and mug; knife, fork and spoon; and the flat iron, which came in useful as a door stop.

There had not been an opportunity to attend lectures on army procedures during our time in Woolwich but, right from the start, I had formed an impression of the QAIMNS that was an entirely good one. For one thing there was very little talk of discipline, but an unspoken presumption that one was a mature and professionally-trained person attached to a distinguished army nursing service which had steadily grown in stature since its beginnings in the era of Florence Nightingale.

In my training days I had been constantly belittled, never praised. I felt I was regarded as useful but expendable. My bruised spirit recovered in the warmth of an encouraging and accepting milieu so that I developed a greater confidence in myself and a new assurance in my work. Once in India the regular sisters were a tremendous help in forming positive attitudes even when the tasks ahead seemed daunting. I don't remember any of them losing their 'cool' even when faced with the admission of a hundred patients in the hot weather.

I settled down with my writing case to inform friends of my change of address. 340 Battery were moving to Budge Budge, which was still within range of Calcutta; Charlie Brown was in Colombo, Ceylon; Dick Amsden in Waziristan; and Major Sealy, my first patient in India, was about to move to a training centre for mountain warfare at Abbothabad on the North West Frontier. Gordon Brock of 293 Battery was at Dum-Dum, an airfield not far from Calcutta.

Matron called the six of us together, informing us that the train journey to Asansol would only take two hours and that we would be met by someone from the 65th Combined Military Hospital at the station. It cannot have been very easy for the Calcutta matron to have had twenty-eight recruits billeted on her without warning, particularly as they were ignorant of the relevance of army forms to every hospital transaction. Add to this the various attractions of a rich social life to lively young women who were restrained from keeping late hours solely by the necessity of having to rise early for duty on the wards, and it can be seen just how unenviable the task of a matron in the regulars could be.

I didn't much mind leaving the quiet residential area of Calcutta where the hospital stood, as it was not very different from the suburbs of any large city. This was not the India that I had come so far to see. Even the teeming life of the dock area, with its pullulating energy, was to be preferred – for a short time at least.

On 29 April we caught the 3pm train for Asansol. We had all reported to the field cashier in order to collect the 50 rupees allowed for travelling expenses. Various inoculations and vaccinations had been performed on us. Sisters Waller, Wyber, Hamilton, McNally, myself and Miss Ferrier, our acting matron, set off on the short train journey to north-west Bengal, not far from the borders of Bihar.

3 · Bengal Posting

Whatever distinction Asansol could lay claim to was by virtue of its position as a railway centre on the route of the Grand Trunk Road from Calcutta to New Delhi, the capital of India. It was ideally situated to control the rich traffic in grain and manufactured goods between heavily populated Calcutta and the fertile wheat-growing areas of the Punjab in the north. The Tropic of Cancer cuts straight through the town, condemning it to seven months of temperatures between 90 and 100 degrees Fahrenheit and five months of variable weather that might become cool around Christmas but was seldom cold.

Asansol was the Crewe of West Bengal. Hundreds of coolies served the railway, keeping it clear of stones and fallen trees, checking the bolts and fish-plates, giving warning of floods which could wash away the soil and creeping home at night to the cheerless coolie lines at the side of the track. The chimneys of the nearby Kulti works belched smoke and steam as steel for the war effort flowed from the furnaces and rolling-mills on to the goods trains at Asansol junction, ready to be carried to the factories of India to be made into armaments or to be exported to industrial centres in the Allied countries.

The Royal Army Medical Corps major who welcomed us at the railway station regretted the absence of a sisters' mess, explaining that the local school buildings had only lately been requisitioned by the medical services to be transformed into a hospital; in the circumstances, he advised us, we would do well to accept the hospitality of the British community of steel managers and their wives at Burnpur, a mile from the hospital. This seemed a more attractive proposition than camping out in the hospital grounds, so we picked up our hand luggage and followed our baggage-laden coolies to a dilapidated bus.

As we rattled along the dusty roads Mary McNally, an attractive red-haired sister whom I knew only slightly, whispered to me, 'If it's a double billet, shall we share?' I just had time to answer 'yes' before the bus drew up outside the biggest bungalow in the area. 'Room for two!' someone called. Mary and I jumped down, waved to the others and hurried across the burning compound into the shade of the porch. The senior steel manager, Mr Linton, a portly, fresh-faced widower in his sixties, greeted us in a friendly manner then introduced us to his second-in-command, Mr Hind, whose thin, delicate wife seemed to be the epitome of all the dreadful things that the Indian climate was supposed to do to women. Later, in the bedroom, I asked Mary how long she thought it would be before we too sank into faded memsahibship but she assured me that it would take at least ten years and the war would hardly last that long.

We drank iced lime juice as we rested on twin beds festooned with the finest white gauze mosquito curtains. The large bedroom led into a well-appointed dressing-room and a bathroom where the flush WC and pink porcelain bath and handbasin filled us with delighted anticipation; no need to extract our unreliable canvas baths from our bedding-rolls in order to wallow in two inches of water as we had done in Calcutta. Mary and I congratulated ourselves on our good fortune; no matter how hard we worked at the hospital there would be a haven of comfort to return to at night. Excitedly we began to unpack our trunks.

At eight o'clock the following morning, tea and arrowroot biscuits were brought to the bedside by a turbanned bearer, whose bare feet made no sound on the polished floor tiles. He handed a note to us on a silver salver informing us that we were not required to report for duty that day but that the ladies of the neighbourhood would call upon us at eleven o'clock. This was to be our first meeting with the memsahibs of India so we were anxious to make a good impression. Mary and I put on the new frocks we had bought in the Calcutta bazaar and sauntered into the loggia for breakfast, sharing our melon-like papaya, toast and marmalade with the wilting and querulous Mrs Hind, who confided to us that she loathed India and longed to be back in her native Nottingham, where she used to teach infants before she married the rather dashing Mr Hind.

When the memsahibs arrived they politely admired our frocks, which were in the same style as they were wearing, but we were quickly made aware that what the expatriate ladies really wanted to see was a frock straight from 'home', no matter

Left to right: Mrs Hind, Mary McNally, Mr Hind, the author
at Mr Linton's bungalow, Asansol, 1942.

how faded and worn the garment might be. Then they would
be able to keep up with the fashions by having a copy made
by the local *durzi* (tailor). I brought out my shabby floral dirndl
dress with the elasticated waist to show them what was being
worn when we left England. They went into raptures over the
style, which would be simplicity itself to copy. These memsahibs were not members of the élite army families who had
become stereotypes in our minds, but cosy middle class women
from the Midlands. They cross-questioned us closely about all
the happenings in wartime Britain, anxious to hear any items
of news, no matter how trivial, even though we protested that
the information was already three months out of date.

I asked them how they occupied themselves, with husbands
out all day producing steel for the war effort and with so many
servants at their disposal. They told us that they wrote to their
children and other relatives in England very often, entertained
each other continually, played mahjong in the evenings and
spent many hours in the swimming pool next door, where we

were invited to join them in our off-duty time. I hesitated to enquire if they would be helping out at the hospital in a voluntary capacity. None of them looked particularly robust, the long years in the less than salubrious Bengal climate having withered the roses from their cheeks.

On the following day an ambulance came to convey us to the hospital. It was a day of brilliant lightning effects, which we watched rather anxiously through the open door of our rickety vehicle, wondering if they were an introduction to the severe thunderstorms we had heard about. After a few minutes the 65th Combined Military Hospital came into view, a cluster of ornate flat-roofed buildings two stories high girded with verandas. The heavy wooden shutters framing the windows and closed on the sides where the sun beat down looked as though they would be totally impervious to heavy monsoon rain. The large compound consisted of stretches of struggling grass and scrubby trees.

A tall major came out of his office to greet us. As he drew closer I noticed that the letters on his shoulder read 'IMS' which, I presumed, stood for Indian Medical Service. He introduced himself to Miss Ferrier and the rest of us as the commanding officer, Major Edward Lossing, then explained that a signal had been sent to warn him that two hundred patients were arriving by train from Assam and that we would have to start ward preparation from scratch. Half-an-hour later we stood in the midst of wooden bedsteads, straw mattresses, wash-bowls, tables, brass ashtrays, report books and army forms of every description, all waiting to be sorted out and transformed by us into something resembling a hospital.

The sun was at its height, burning like copper in a cobalt sky. Even though the Indian coolies and sepoy orderlies did all the physical work, our clothes were soaked with sweat merely in the process of organising everything. Before we came off duty at 8pm we were satisfied with the arrangements for the reception of sick and wounded men. One of the Indian orderlies had even found time to pluck a sprig of bougainvillaea, which he put in a tin on the ward desk.

With the arrival of our patients came news of the fall of Mandalay on 2 May so the Japanese threat to India was real. Most of our new arrivals in the wards were medical cases — at that time there were over a hundred sickness casualties to every one wounded, the majority suffering from malaria. I supposed that the more severely wounded patients would be flown out from the Assam border to hospitals like the 21st British General Hospital, Calcutta, or to Poona and Ranchi, which were well-established and fully-equipped.

The stories the soldiers told of the retreat from Burma were depressing indeed. The monsoon started earlier than it did in India; heavy showers had impeded the weary marchers, depressed by defeat, hungry and fever-ridden, as they followed the muddy tracks day after day until they reached the comparative safety of Imphal. British, Indian and Gurkha troops, distinguished solely by the identity discs round their necks — we never knew their units — shared a brotherhood of emaciated raggedness.

Soon we began to receive a thin trickle of sunstroke cases, which grew to a flood as the heat increased. Unfortunately I was in such a state of exhaustion myself during that first experience of working long hours in the Indian hot weather season that I sometimes neglected my nightly diary, falling into a restless sleep as soon as my head touched the pillow. I did enter the fact that five patients were dying of heat-stroke on 23 May, but the number who died in the end was twelve or thirteen. Dozens of others, diagnosed in the early stages, survived, one man recovering after his temperature had registered 110 degrees Fahrenheit though he may well have suffered permanent brain damage.

The basic cause of heat collapse (also known as heat apoplexy or heat exhaustion) was the loss of large quantities of fluid from the body in sweat, carrying with it essential salt and trace elements. The chemical balance was disturbed, the temperature rose rapidly and the patient lost consciousness. Every effort was made to bring the fever down to 101 degrees Fahrenheit but no further, as it then descended so rapidly that death ensued.

An entry from my diary — written on my day off — illustrates how drastic were the measures taken to reduce the temperature of heat stroke victims:

There are now sixty-five patients in the medical ward. My heart sinks when I see yet another casualty brought in on a stretcher. All these deaths are having a bad effect on the morale of the rest of the patients in the ward. The dramatic treatment of wringing out sheets in a tin bath of ice-water and wrapping them round the patient in full view of everyone (there is no room for screens even if we had them) must be having a depressing effect on the others as it is frequently followed by the death of the patient. Can the heat get any worse? It is said that it will be even hotter next month before the monsoon rains.

Shortly after the beginning of May, the promised terrific thunderstorms and gales heralded by continuous lightning had subsided. They were the tail-end of the spring rains, which were welcomed by the agricultural Indians as germinators of their seeds and waterers of fruit, vegetable and grain crops. With the prospect of new life in the earth came my first experience of the death of someone I knew personally. Dick Burton wrote from Calcutta that Mitch had died of heat-stroke. My anger and distress knew no bounds. If only I had still been with my friends of 340 Battery, I thought, I would have noticed the first symptoms and Mitch might have been saved. That night I was unable to sleep and lay in the stuffy darkness, mourning the man whom I looked on as a brother. I planned the letter I would write to Dick and the others, deciding that I would ask for a weekend leave as soon as I reasonably could in order to see them all.

Mary and I were the first sisters to move into Success Villa when it was purchased for the hospital by Major Lossing. We had been very happy at Mr Linton's bungalow. He had given us the use of his air-conditioned room when we returned over-fatigued from duty; but the ambulance drive back and forward, sometimes twice daily, was very time-consuming and wearisome in the heat, which increased steadily day by day. The memsahibs gave a farewell party for us, where we learned that one or two of them had joined the St John Ambulance Brigade in order to help out at the hospital. However, there was one delicate plant who, when the sisters returned from working a ten-hour day (which we did twice weekly at that time), would fan herself and say in a faint voice, 'I'm absolutely exhausted. I've written two letters home to England today!'

It was pleasant to have a bedroom and small bathroom to myself in Success Villa, a whitewashed bungalow on the Grand Trunk Road but still within the hospital compound. In one of the large leafy trees outside my window a colony of egrets, their plumage dazzling white from below, kept up a constant harsh squawking as they preened and fluttered, the crests on their heads rising and falling like geishas' fans. Cormorants, black as night, occupied a neighbouring tree, filling the air with a powerful fishy odour.

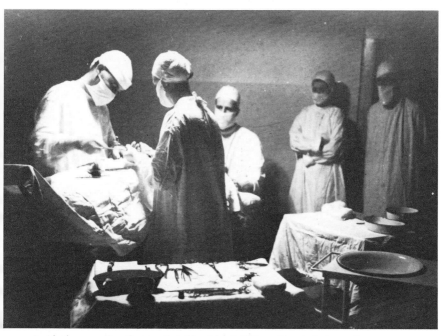

Inside the operating theatre, 65th Combined Military Hospital, Asansol, October 1942. Captain Wilson RAMC operates, assisted by Sister Mary McNally QAIMNS. Major Rogerson RAMC is the anaesthetist.

Mary and I had got on quite well together but I can't say that we were bosom friends. We were both independent characters and I think we respected each other's personalities, but there the likeness ended. She was tougher than I, with a veneer of charm that was apt to crack under pressure, revealing an underlying maliciousness that could be amusing but was sometimes cruel. Mary put me in mind of Scarlett O'Hara in *Gone with the Wind*, which I was reading at the time. She even resembled Vivien Leigh, who played the part of Scarlett in the film. I thought her gem-hard and a born survivor.

What was quite certain was that her training at the Brighton Royal Infirmary had made her into an excellent theatre sister. She worked in conditions of incredible discomfort in the makeshift operating room, whose windows had to be kept shut to exclude dust-borne bacteria. Being fair-skinned and auburn-haired, she was afflicted more than most people with prickly heat, which produced a burning rash on her face, chest and arms and made work in that closed atmosphere intolerable. Captain Wilson RAMC, the surgeon, shared her misery, sweating so much that the moisture from his forehead was in danger of splashing into his patients' wounds even though an orderly continually swabbed his brow. The bandanna which he was driven to wearing round his head needed to be changed frequently. Mary used to say that Major Wilson was a very good surgeon and had been at one of the London hospitals. Who gave the anaesthetics at that time I cannot imagine as Major Rogerson, the anaesthetist, only arrived in August.

One day Mary reached the end of her tether. She had had a wretched night with the prickly heat, a robber had stolen 200 rupees from her trunk while she was out at work the previous day and her application for a short leave had been turned down. She did not burst into tears – that was not Mary's way – but she stormed round her room, throwing her sandals out of the window, to the gardener's alarm, and shouted angrily: 'I shall never go back to that terrible theatre. I've had enough. They must find someone else. I just can't take any more!'

Through the window went hairbrush, mirror and vanity case, skimming the *mali*'s head and causing a commotion among the cormorants. But it was all to no avail; Mary was the only trained theatre sister out of the six of us and could not be replaced. An emergency appendix was admitted to the ward that very afternoon and poor Mary had to swallow her exasperation and present herself for duty.

The combination of extreme heat, overwork and unaccustomed germs took its toll of the QAs that first summer. We were often ill or below par with sore throats, intestinal upsets and low fevers. While serving the patients' lunch one day I felt on the point of collapse and had to retire to Success Villa, where Mary came to tell me that there was a king cobra curled up in the mortuary. I felt that I might well be sharing the accommodation of that sacred serpent in the near future, these morbid fancies being engendered by a fever, a sore throat and a severe attack of laryngitis.

I was admitted to the small civil hospital for a few days, but even in my misery I thought it strange that the CO should visit me three times each day. Could I really be a candidate for the mortuary slab? As I gradually returned to my customary good health and the visits continued I began to look with curiosity at this quiet man. I had heard that he was a Canadian from Ontario who had spent the last eight years in the Indian Medical Service. He looked middle-aged to me; experience of the climate had taught him to move at a leisurely pace, wasting as little effort as possible, which made him appear older than his thirty-four years. His eyes were sad in expression but of a clear, candid blue. When he smiled, a feat he performed for me when he heard the curious sounds that came from my convalescent larynx, his face was transformed. He actually looked quite young.

Major Robbie Niblock, the civil surgeon, paid a call with his wife in order to invite me to dinner on the day I left his hospital. They were typical of the Scots couples of a certain age to be found in commercial and professional circles all over India. He, thickset, sandy-haired, equable; she, comely in a plump fashion, hospitable and fond of animals. They both played golf daily, fished whenever they could find enough water and were the leading lights in every social activity. Jean Niblock ran the St John Ambulance classes, recruiting Anglo-Indian girls for the military hospital.

When I walked the short distance to the Niblocks' large bungalow and entered the sitting-room, whose furniture looked as though it had been carved from the teak of the Burmese jungles, I found that the only other guest was Major Lossing. I was slightly taken aback but managed to disguise my reaction; my still-hoarse voice gave me the excuse to say very little but my mind was working overtime. I was both intrigued and wary.

At the end of the evening it was naturally assumed that the major should see me back to Success Villa on the way to his own rooms at the end of the surgical block a few minutes' walk away. Before he said goodnight, he asked me if I would join him for a meal at the station restaurant the following week. I wondered what matron would think — after all he was the commanding officer of the hospital. It could be embarrassing for her. I said I would let him know and whisked indoors to avoid further discussion.

Miss Ferrier, one of the regular QA sisters as opposed to wartime reserves like ourselves, was still our matron at this time. Being plain, sallowed by the sun and gentle in her manner, she reminded me of an older version of my friend Anne Richardson. She came from an army family in which it was traditional for at least one unmarried daughter to join the Army Nursing Service. Miss Ferrier was actually a member of the Indian branch of the service, the Indian Medical Nursing Service, which in 1902 had been amalgamated with the British QAs under the Royal Warrant of Queen Alexandra. The IMNS sisters wore our badge with the inscription *Sub Cruce Candida* on their scarlet shoulder capes.

When I spoke to matron about Major Lossing's invitation to dinner, she hesitated and I knew exactly what was going through her head. If she said that I should refuse, when other sisters and medical officers were fraternising happily off duty, then it would look as though the CO was being victimised. If she advised me to accept I would be required to behave in a very discreet manner – off-duty and on-duty attitudes being kept in separate compartments. She finally decided I was to be allowed to accept the invitation but added the rider that I was to be guided by the opinions of Dr and Mrs Niblock, who were great friends of Major Lossing. When I told Mary McNally about matron's verdict she was highly amused. 'No one else but you would have bothered to ask permission,' she said. 'Have a good time!'

Miss Ferrier lent a sympathetic ear to our exasperated complaints about 'Bunny' Austin, the doctor in charge of the skin ward. With the increase in prickly heat the condition of soldiers and airmen already afflicted with such ailments as chronic eczema, psoriasis and dhobi's itch deteriorated. Only by transferring the sufferers to a cool climate or immuring them in an air-conditioned room could their symptoms be alleviated. Many people used mild antiseptics to relieve the irritation but some latent artistic impulse in Bunny caused him to conduct extensive trials using the only other recognised treatment – the external application of aniline dyes. This Billy Bunter of a major, who himself suffered grievously from copious sweating with its resultant prickly heat, always looked as though he had just taken a shower in his bush jacket and shorts. Strangely enough, with all that sweating he never seemed to lose weight. Rumour had it that he came from one of the distinguished London hospitals and that they had sent him out East for experience.

Each of his patients, wearing only a loincloth, had his body divided into four equal parts, which Bunny marked with a pen according to colour. Under the critical eye of the master draughtsman, the orderlies stepped forward to paint in the four sections with gentian violet, mercurachrome red, acriflavine yellow and vibrant green. What was infuriating about this ritual was that nothing rubbed off on to Bunny himself. Not a spot of experimental colour enlivened his pallid dripping countenance or clothes, whereas everyone else involved had to contend with patches of irremovable dye on sheets, towels and garments.

But our tribulations were as nothing compared with those of Bunny's patients. These colourful fellows, who in their rainbow resplendence would have put to shame a witch-doctor from an aboriginal tribe, tried to hide from the light of day because, when the news of Major Austin's artistic endeavours got around, there was a constant stream of sight-seeing visitors from all over the hospital, each with some plausible excuse for looking in on the skin ward. Bunny's eyes would glisten with enthusiasm behind his wire-framed spectacles as he discussed the relative merits of his dyes with anyone who would listen, dragging forward his unwilling works of art to expatiate on a leg here or an arm there which he insisted showed definite signs of improvement. It was all to no effect. Most of the skin patients had to go on suffering stoically, only being removed to a cooler climate if the weeks or months they spent in hospital caused them to be a liability to the army.

Despite the different climatic conditions there was very little change from ward routine as practised at home. I doubt if any of the men, except for those in the combat areas, would have accepted an eight-hour day in the hot weather, week after week, month after month, as the sisters did. Our hours of duty were no different from what they would have been in England and remained that way until the war was over. The day staff came on duty at 8am to take the report of the patients' condition; then the diet sheets had to be attended to so that the quartermaster-sergeant could give instructions to the kitchen staff with regard to the type and amounts of food to be supplied. I personally found the army diets to be incredibly complicated, never having been used to a system which allowed half-an-ounce of tea and three-quarters of an ounce of sugar to patients on 'subsistence' diets on admission and demanded forecasts of all other diets as to quantity and variety.

At 9am came the sister's round of the ward with an orderly. It was then that the value of the sister's long training came into its own; a few words with the patient, a glance at his chart and the sister or doctor could gauge accurately his disposition both physical and mental. It was an ability that came with experience and could not be learned any other way.

The rest of the morning was taken up with dressings, medicines and four-hourly treatments carried out by sisters and orderlies. The Indian sweeper saw to the bedpans, the *bhiste*,

Officers' ward, 65th Combined Military Hospital, Asansol, July 1943.
Captain Rennie (left), the author, Lieutenant-Colonel Edward Lossing.

who was often affectionately addressed as Gunga Din, to the
lime juice. This was made in huge earthenware *chattis*, which
dripped coolingly in their wooden frames at the end of every
ward.

Evening ward routine was a repeat of the morning's work
but by then numbers of the British patients would have had
airgraphs or letters from home; there might be photos of wives
and babies to admire and the sayings of children to listen to.
A wind-up gramophone would be taken outside to entertain
all within hearing with its lively tunes, which mingled strangely
with the pipe and drum music from the Indian lines. Some of
the convalescents might attempt a Fred Astaire dance routine
or waltz around holding an imaginary partner, singing 'South
of the Border' or 'Wish me Luck as you Wave me Goodbye',
much to the bashful delight of the Indian sweeper and *bhiste*.

To this accompaniment my evening report would be written, commenting on the condition of the ill patients, ready for the night sister who took over at 8pm. Occasionally we stayed on duty all day, suffering the intense afternoon heat, but finishing at 6pm. Once a week we were allowed a whole day free – unless a convoy of patients came in, in which case everyone returned to help. There were times when Mary and I went back to our billet so exhausted by the heat that we could not face a meal and made do with mango fool, a mixture of ripe mangoes, sugar and cream which the cook kept in the icebox for us.

In the hospital grounds tents were set up for those with infectious fevers, such as smallpox, in order to keep them isolated from the main blocks. The communual cookhouse was a large *basha* made of bamboo and reeds. A pile of discarded chicken entrails was placed strategically outside the wire-gauze screen to attract the hundreds of flies, which would otherwise have waited for the swing-doors to open. The wood and coir-rope *charpoys* (bedsteads) were havens of rest for the ubiquitous bugs, which made the patients' lives intolerable at night by their blood-sucking habits. The only way to get rid of them was to boil the bedsteads. To this end Major Lossing had a brick-supported water tank built, under which a fire could be lit. Indian sepoys, looking like devils dealing with damned souls in a medieval fresco, stood by with clouds of steam rising around them ready to push the beds under the water until all the bugs were destroyed.

Another duty which devolved upon the CO was the shooting of stray pariah dogs, which were drawn to the hospital compound by the smell of food. They were a constant danger to health as they could carry rabies and flea-borne diseases. Major Lossing was a familiar sight in the evening, stalking his prey like a long-legged heron, with a cringing pariah dog trotting ahead and glancing round frequently to gauge the distance between itself and the man with the gun. An Indian sweeper trailing a burial sack brought up the rear. Nature in her evolutionary capacity was already helping to cope with the manifestly unfit. I once watched a pack of pai dogs set upon a diseased puppy and maul it to death.

16 June 1942

I have been out quite often with Teddy. Although his name
is Edward I have decided to call him that. Dr and Mrs
Niblock joined us after tea, when we went to fish in the
tank – an artificial pond of water about one hundred yards
long, rectangular and surrounded by banks of earth – but
all we caught was a bony mudfish. The Indians use the tank
for washing their animals as the river is too far away for
them to walk to. It was a perfect evening; the sky was
lemon and egg-shell blue with smokey clouds. The new
moon rose at six o'clock and later the sky was thick with
huge stars, some of them shooting across the sky. There are
five spaniel puppies at the Niblocks. They were whining –
perhaps because the air is so stifling and humid.

The reason that the heat was particularly trying was that the
monsoon rains were approaching. We had been sweltering in
temperatures of 90–100 degrees Fahrenheit with everybody
becoming more short-tempered each day. Our nerves tingled
with the peacock cry of the brain-fever bird. Its harsh screaming
started at the bottom of the scale and rose higher in a loud
shrieking arpeggio of sound time after time, hour after hour,
gaining it the reputation of driving men mad in the hot weather.
We began to hate the sun, seeing its dreadful orange eye rise
out of the earth relentlessly, ready to scorch our skins off. The
whole countryside appeared to be panting as mirage-like reflec-
tions hovered in the distorted air. We heard the low menacing
growls of thunder as the cloud piled up on the horizon while
the oppressive heat grew more and more unbearable. Only the
water-buffaloes seemed resigned to the drought, content to wallow deeply in the river mud, covered up to the nose-tip to protect their dry, thin-haired hides.

18 June 1942

Today the rains came. In the small hours it happened. First
I heard a distant whispering like the sound the sweeper
makes when he uses a broom of grasses to sweep the loggia,
then a susurration as though a hundred trees were blowing
together and finally there came a deluge whose sound
drowned every note in the universe. You could hear, see,
smell and feel nothing but rain! I felt drunk on rain and as

there was nobody about I ran outside, letting it sluice down my body, shouting for joy as loud as I could because nobody could hear anything above the steady, rolling, drum-beat of the rain.

But the damp heat proved to be as hard, if not harder, to bear as the dry heat; it was more enervating. We were frequently drenched just crossing over from one ward to another as it was quite impossible to wear any form of waterproofing or coat in that climate. Wellington boots hidden in the bottom of steel trunks from our Oxford days came into use for sloshing about in the mud. All our books and records turned green with mildew; everything smelt of toadstools and food went mouldy. I'm afraid we began to murmur about our tribulations again like the Israelites in the wilderness. Many people carried umbrellas everywhere, particularly *babus* (clerks) and *munshis* (teachers), while the poorer Indians wrapped their heads in cotton cloths and looked miserable.

The rains brought out the creepy-crawlies from their hiding places. It was always wise to check the hole in the bathroom wall where the water from your tin bath drained away, to make sure a snake wasn't lurking there. The wooden commodes harboured centipedes of a large size and assorted spiders, but it was surprising how quickly one got used to them. Sudden terrifying storms burst upon us every few days, flooding our rooms and changing the burnt brown landscape into a luxuriant green Eden where conditions were ideal for the growth of succulent tropical fruits.

When I went out to dinner with the Niblocks and Teddy again, wearing a blue crêpe frock, the front became soaked with rain as I ran to the porch. The skirt shrank, rising well above my knees at a time when nobody had envisaged mini-skirts. My hostess wrapped me in a voluminous dressing gown and in that *déshabillé* I appeared before the company.

Together with the monsoon rains came our first letters from England, some of them dated three months earlier. Once they started to arrive they poured in in shoals; everyone you met had his or her nose buried in a piece of paper, limiting conversation to grunts or groans with an occasional 'ah'. Heavily censored as they were, the air letters gave us no information about the war, but family photos without any background of bombed buildings were allowed, providing a source of great comfort and pleasure. There was a letter from Aunt Madge in my mail

87

telling me her son Peter was in the RAF somewhere in India and insisting that I 'go over to see him' – as though India were the size of Southport.

In mid-July I asked matron if I could have a long weekend in Calcutta, a request that was willingly granted. My hair had grown so long that I had to tie it back under my veil, making a visit to the hairdresser top priority. Also I needed to stock up with soap, toothpaste and shampoo of a reasonable quality, to say nothing of talcum powder, face powder and lipstick.

Calcutta was its old familiar suffocating self, though the Grand Hotel where I stayed was cool enough. During a siesta on the first day I heard the sound of singing in the street, a woman's voice intoning a sad, pleading melody over and over again. When I leaned from the window I saw a young beggar woman, with a kohl-eyed baby on her hip, smiling up at me with hand cupped for baksheesh. I dropped some annas into her outstretched sari, after which she held up the baby for me to see. I presumed her pitch was a bundle of rags on a pavement somewhere, with prostitution as her only means of livelihood. I wondered if it were true that families actually mutilated their children so that they would arouse pity in the bystander, who might be prompted to offer alms. There were certainly a great many disabled children. Had I not been inured by my training to the tragedies of life I could not have faced Calcutta; even so, a sense of guilt haunted me when I passed the alleys swarming with destitute people.

Out in the main thoroughfare, Chowringhee, I watched the Sikh taxi drivers with their untidy pink turbans like overblown roses charging among the rickshaws and crowded buses in a suicidal frenzy, fingers pressed relentlessly on their klaxon horns. I paid one of them a couple of rupees to take me to the Hooghly River where the ships come in, which reminded me of the Port of London.

On leaving the Grand Hotel next morning I ran into Sister Copping, the rosy-cheeked, dark-haired girl from Yorkshire who had sung 'Linden Lea' on the *Monarch of Bermuda*. With her was the blonde, extremely shy Mary King, who I thought had the most beautiful face of all the women on the ship, yet who shrank from any social gathering. The men considered her colourless and proud but I noticed one day that she had a slight limp, which no doubt discouraged her from dancing and made her self-conscious. They gave me the news that Doris Oliver, my old friend, was on leave so I did not call at the

Chowringhee Road, Calcutta, 1944.

once-familiar British General Hospital where they were all working.

In the afternoon Dick Burton arrived to take me to Budge-Budge where I found 340 Battery living in fairly primitive conditions. Colonel Ken Hargreaves, who was now commanding 3rd Indian Anti-Aircraft Brigade, was no longer their CO. They had not yet seen any action, which made them feel dispirited and superfluous. Later they were used to instruct Indians from Madras as artillerymen, but like many thousands of our troops in India who were involved in training Indians and guarding air bases and supplies they possibly never heard a shot fired in anger. All of them had lost weight; none thought much of India. They gave me a photo of Mitch and saw me off on the Asansol train. I never met any of them again except for Dick, who left Bombay for home at the same time as I did.

On the train I wrote in my diary:

What a relief to leave the smells and sights of Calcutta. It was good to talk to Charles again and I was interested in what he had to say about the arch-villain (from the British point of view) Subhas Chandra Bose. He is far more impatient than Gandhi and wants independence straight away even if he has to foment trouble amongst the population and side with the Japanese to put pressure on the British.

The other thing that concerned me in Calcutta was the plight of those rickshaw wallahs. Charles said that they had very short lives because they work on so little food and are riddled with diseases such as hook worm and tuberculosis. I saw both Indians and Europeans kick out at puny little men who pull them along in rickshaws to make them go faster. It would give me great pleasure to put such bullies between the shafts and drive them for miles through the crowded streets so that they would know how it felt to be a rickshaw wallah.

Throughout the months of July and August there was an increase of patients suffering from the diseases that are the scourge of India. The British dysentery ward held more than fifty servicemen; there were a few typhoid cases who had to be isolated on the open portico of the medical area; and benign and malignant malaria took their inexorable toll. Indian and British troops were in separate wards with their own orderlies, whose work was supervised by the sisters. The officer patients were provided with small rooms flanked by a wide veranda where they played chess or cards while convalescing.

Edward Lossing, now a lieutenant-colonel, found it necessary to commandeer several buildings adjacent to the hospital in order to accommodate the overflow of patients. During the exercise he rescued a perfectly good refrigerator, which transformed life in the medical ward, housing in its capacious depths ice-cubes, cordials, goat's milk and eggs. Although the earthenware *chattis* kept lime juice really cold, it was heartening to be able to give iced drinks to ill patients.

When the time for my three weeks' night duty came up I had to take leave of the magnificent fridge and cross over to the Indian block. The Indian wards were a revelation to me. I came face to face with strange diseases I had never heard of. Infestation with guinea worm, the oldest known human parasite, which the orderlies twisted round a small stick as it issued from the muscle of the leg, was quite common; elephantiasis, caused by another parasitic worm carried by mosquitoes, was rarer but devastating in its later stages. The affected part – usually the foot – grew to enormous proportions and resembled the leg of an elephant, hence the popular name for the condition. Tuberculosis was rife. I once turned the pillow of a terminal case of this illness and found a lump of black, putty-like material. I asked the old man what it was but he grew very excited, clawing at my hand. The Indian orderly said laconically, 'Opium, sister sahib. He die happy!' I quickly tucked it back beneath his pillow.

Night duty on the Indian wards was made more hazardous by intruders from the animal kingdom. The dry rustle of leaves outside the window might presage a rat or a snake going about its lawful business. Flying ants caught in your hair as they whirled under a veranda lamp, then descended to crawl away into the undergrowth leaving thousands of discarded wings glistening on the ground. Geckos advertised their presence with a squeak as they tried to bite each other's tails off, sometimes falling to the floor with a squelchy sound.

An Indian *chokidar* (night-watchman) walked before me with a hurricane lamp when I visited the outlying tents of patients with infectious diseases. He was so nervous that he kept up a continual loud-voiced singing, hoping to frighten away such nocturnal marauders as jackals, snakes and tigers. One dark night he suddenly stopped singing, dropped his lamp, which promptly extinguished itself, and ran off, leaving me in pitch darkness with the growing conviction that there was a snake before me on the path. I backed away slowly, feeling for the trunks of trees that lined the rough track, then turned and staggered through the mud to the nearest ward. The unfortunate *chokidar* was dismissed for drunkenness. To the Indian personnel, all snakes were poisonous kraits or king cobras, but I only remember one case of snake-venom poisoning that night duty and the patient survived.

My most alarming experience came at three o'clock one morning when a sepoy from the *pagal* (psychiatric) ward crept into my duty room armed with a menacing pickaxe taken from the fire-protection stand and advanced towards me. Instinctively I snatched the fly spray from my desk and pumped it vigorously in his direction. He turned and fled silently down the veranda, to be intercepted by his orderly.

Although I could not communicate with Indians in their own languages I made contact through the splendid orderlies, who all appeared to have a smattering of several tongues. Abdul

Bahadur from Allahabad was one of these. He would stand among a group of patients as they sat outside in the cool of the evening smoking *biris* and say expansively, 'Sister sahib, what you wish to know?' I would ask him what the patients liked to eat, what they thought of the army and – the question they liked best – how many children they had. Thus I discovered how fraught with uncertainty was their life in the agricultural villages; how their debts, passing from father to son, weighed them down; and how few of their children survived infancy.

After working on the Indian wards I began to take more notice of the people in the area of Asansol where Mary and I did our shopping. There were booths along the street of the bazaar where leather or snakeskin shoes could be made within a few hours – even riding-boots would be attempted but they were not an unqualified success. Everybody crowded round in a friendly fashion when we made a purchase, too polite to stare directly but watching covertly through their conveniently long eyelashes. There was no pushing and shouting and demands for baksheesh as in Calcutta.

Further down the street there was a resident *durzi* sitting cross-legged on the ground by an ancient Singer sewing machine and leafing through paper dress patterns that might have been left behind by some pre-war memsahib. Mary and I examined the beautiful nightdress materials: pale blue chiffon, white georgette and peach-coloured triple ninon, lavishly spending forty rupees each. The *durzi* polished his spectacles, shooed a small boy away from his important customers and spread out his tattered nightgown patterns for our approval. A few days later the finished garments were delivered to Success Villa carefully wrapped in a spotless cotton cloth.

Apart from the Burnpur and Kulti Clubs the railway station restaurant was the only eating-place for Europeans. The Hindus and Muslims had their own separate establishments further down the platform. The railway restaurant's choice of food was limited to three dishes – omelette, curry and bacon-and-eggs. It was rather a dreary place and with so much transit traffic passing through the station bringing impatient, preoccupied customers, the bearers became off-hand and bored. Fortunately for those of us with a sweet tooth there was Madath's, a store run by an Armenian whose speciality was a glass of fizzy lemonade containing a block of ice-cream that melted away so fast that one had to drink it through a straw.

A village street, Bengal, 1944.

A concert hall called the Indian Institute showed quite up-to-date American films such as *Blood and Sand*, starring Tyrone Power, and *A Woman's Face*, with Joan Crawford as the main attraction. Everyone ate peanuts or chewed betel-nut, and when we stood up to sing 'God Save the King' our feet crunched noisily on shells and husks. To return by rickshaw to the hospital compound at night after a film was a pleasurable experience. Blue smoke from burning cow dung hung on the air, blurring the oil lamps which illuminated each booth along the narrow street. On a pile of leaves under a sandalwood tree a naked bearded sadhu of the Brahmin Bairagi sect, grey with ash, said his evening prayers. The soft, persistent tinkle of the rickshaw bell started an echo in your brain that lingered for years.

The long hot summer burnt itself out at last. With the end of the rains and the start of the cooler weather in October the number of admissions to the hospital fell. We had time to speculate on what the Japanese were up to, but all the officers could tell us was that nobody fought in the jungle during the monsoon season because of the mud and mosquitoes. Now that the weather had improved, they assured us, there would be some action.

People with such titles as 'Deputy Director of Medical Services' began to visit the hospital. Miss Ferrier left and was replaced by Matron Tobin, a plump, rosy-faced Irishwoman, easy-going and good-tempered, who never hurried for anyone. For dinner in the mess she appeared in the splendid scarlet wool shoulder cape of the regulars, which we reserves regarded with envy even though they were stiflingly hot to wear. Some matrons wore them all through the summer season, when their faces became as scarlet as their capes. Considering that she was over fifty, Miss Tobin stood up to the climate very well. Her lovely cat, Mrs Honey, produced three kittens who lived in a basket in the sisters' mess, providing a source of delight and amusement for us all.

Miss Tobin and Colonel Lossing escorted an elderly general round the wards early in November. I was in charge of the British dysentery ward, where a few days before I had distributed some Christmas decorations for the patients to work on. When the inspection party was seen in the distance all the convalescent men jumped into bed and sat at attention. As we started on our tour of the ward, after having met the general, I was mortified to see that Private Watkins from the Royal Army Ordnance Corps camp at Nursa in the second bed was wearing a jolly, red-faced Father Christmas mask which made him look remarkably like the general. The general stared straight at him, remarking to Miss Tobin in a loud voice how healthy the men appeared to be. He was getting on in years and I wasn't sure whether he had noticed this breach of discipline; but as he started to go down the stone steps that led from the ward he turned to me and winked.

12 November 1942

Chinese commander-in-chief, with a general and a colonel, are in the officers' ward. They were in a car accident on the Grand Trunk Road but they are not badly hurt – merely shaken. It is all very hush-hush.

I was curious to know who the senior Chinese officer was and wandered along the veranda of the private ward to try and catch a glimpse of him, but there was a British sergeant on duty and all the doors were shut. I even went so far as to ask Teddy if it was General Chiang Kai-shek, perhaps on his way to a conference in Delhi or Calcutta, but of course he wouldn't tell me.

All these straws in the wind indicated renewed Allied activity in the near future. This supposition was reinforced when more doctors and nurses were posted to our hospital to enable matron to send her hard-pressed staff on leave.

We had already been making the most of the cooler evenings to go by truck to the River Damodar a mile or two away from Asansol, taking along a wind-up gramophone, some records and a rug to lounge on. There for the first time I heard a recording of the great cellist Pablo Casals playing Fauré's 'Après un Rêve', an experience that made such an impression on me that when I hear that plaintive melody so many years afterwards I am wafted back to a moonlit river-bank, with a vista of distant mountains and romantic memories of my first real love affair. But in India one always swings between the earth and the stars. As I closed the lid of the gramophone I saw the busy scarab beetle rolling its ball of dung along the ground to a place of safety.

When possible a mixed group of hospital staff went on leave together, neither the army nor the matrons being too keen on young sisters wandering about India even in pairs. Captain Murray RAMC, a model officer in his knife-edged shorts and spotless bush shirts, who wore his peaked army cap throughout the hot weather and never seemed to sweat, volunteered to escort Sisters Waller and Wyber to Kashmir for a fortnight. These two friends, both high-coloured brunettes, one from a public school the other from a simple country background in Scotland, were seldom seen apart until one of them – Sister Wyber, I believe – got married in Gauhati two years later. Mary McNally departed to Darjeeling with a friend. Teddy, who knew a married couple on leave in Gopalpur, invited me to accompany him there. On reaching Calcutta we were held up for two days because the Madras mail train was not running – a common happening in wartime India. We decided to stay at the Grand Hotel as it was central and as pleasant a place as could be imagined in the cool weather when there was no danger of cholera. After a meal that was superior to anything I had eaten in six months, I retired to bed in the unaccustomed luxury of a curtained room with a real mattress and a down pillow. At two o'clock in the morning I woke up feeling decidedly itchy. I switched on the bedside lamp, illuminating dozens of little black specks on the bottom sheet which scuttled away before my horrified gaze.

Although I had often been bitten by bugs when sitting in cane chairs in public buildings I had never actually seen one before. Fortunately they did not appear to carry disease. I took a bath and spent the rest of the night huddled in an armchair wrapped in a blanket. In the morning I went to complain to the management. The clerk took action but didn't seem particularly surprised. His apology and the offer of a free night's lodging upheld me until the arrival of the Madras mail train.

Gopalpur was a small fishing village on the Bay of Bengal. The journey down the coast of Orissa to the nearest railway station, Berhampur, took sixteen hours. As we approached the end of our ride, curious cone-shaped hills appeared at the side of the track, a joy to the heart after the flat, dusty, parched Asansol plain. The air became fresher with a salt tang to it and I felt like a child returning to the seaside holidays of my youth. A donkey cart ambled along the six miles that took us from Berhampur station to Yatton Hall. It was a long dusty road but paradise was at the end of it.

A row of huts faced the sea, providing cool sleeping accommodation. Meals were served at the stone-built main building. *Chota hazri* (morning tea) could be taken outside at little tables in the privacy of one's own coconut palms. On the first morning a friendly donkey – the one that had pulled us from the station – with his long ears pushed through two holes in a battered straw hat came to greet us, graciously accepting an unripe banana from the breakfast tray, while his owner, as a gesture of appreciation, shinned up a palm tree and threw down a coconut. He then descended, using rope foot-loops, chopped off the thick outer husk of the nut with a machete, pierced the growing end in two places and proceeded to pour the delicious milk into our glasses; after which he salaamed politely and wandered off with the donkey in tow.

The sea along this stretch of coast was very rough with a strong undertow. No visitor was allowed to bathe without lifeguards in attendance. Two local Indians, shiny and wet as seals, held you by either hand and led you into the water, men and women alike. Once they had escorted you beyond the wild waves, they would let you go but bobbed up and down in the sea close by to make sure that the current didn't carry you away. Women were provided with palm-leaf beach huts as changing-rooms and shelters from the noonday sun. The climate at this

A village shop, Bengal, 1944.

time of the year was suitable for sunbathing and, for the first time in India, I acquired a magnificent tan.

The sunrise over the Bay of Bengal was every bit as flamboyant as Kipling described it in his poem 'Mandalay', but we saw something else across the bay that was rather terrifying. It was a waterspout, a great column of water drawn up into the air by the wind meeting another column dipping down from the low cloud and whirling round as it moved across the ocean at a terrific pace. We watched anxiously to see which way it was travelling, feeling very relieved when it made for the coast higher up towards Calcutta, where we hoped it would shed its load of water harmlessly over the Sunderbans. It was the time of year when the south-west monsoons, which scour the Bay of Bengal in a contra-clockwise direction, are replaced by north-east monsoons, which move in a clockwise curve, causing severe storms and flooding on the coast and islands of the bay.

As Gopalpur was a fishing village most of the guests, including Teddy and me, made it their business to be on the beach when the men drifted in with their catch, watching fascinated as the still-sparkling fish slithered into shallow palm-leaf containers ready to be carried up to the hotel for breakfast. The fisherman wore curious little pixie hats of woven straw and very little else. I have never before or since tasted anything so delicious as that fish straight from the sea at Gopalpur. It was served twice a day and nobody ever complained.

On the last day Teddy, his friends the Parkers from Madras and I went for a walk through the pine woods, where we watched a hawk swoop down and fly off with a snake writhing in its beak. It looked hieratic, symbolic of good or evil, and sent a shiver down my spine. We walked along the shore-line, avoiding the scavenger crows who were pecking at a jellyfish, hopping about stiff-legged like vultures round a rotting corpse in the plains. Teddy pointed across the bay in the direction of the Arakan Yoma where, he said, a counter-attack was about to begin against the Japanese. It was not pleasant to think about the war again after ten days of escapism.

When we returned to Asansol, where two of the newcomers, Captain Sadler RAMC and a regular sister, Miss Bevan, had been helping to run the hospital while Miss Tobin took some leave, we heard the news that the Americans, who had been up in the north of Assam, were taking over local sites. There was definitely something brewing.

Meanwhile there were the Christmas preparations to think about. This was the first Christmas away from home for most of our patients and we felt we must make it a good one. There was certainly no problem about the food. Goodies poured in from all directions, particularly from the Red Cross, who were renowned for their tinned fruit cake. Private Watkins, that irrepressible little Geordie, got his pals together and decorated the ward. He had been cured of his bacillary dysentery once but had managed to have another bout of it just before Christmas. I found several of the patients making mistletoe under his direction – little balls of cotton wool stuck on leafy twigs from the compound. Mary, myself and Sister Tuck, who looked very like her namesake Friar Tuck in her girth and rosy complexion, went down to the bazaar on the day before Christmas to buy nuts and dried fruit, then made trifles in the afternoon. Those sisters and doctors who were off duty went to a midnight service and it was 2.30am when we got to bed.

Christmas Day in the dysentery ward, 65th Combined Military Hospital, Asansol, 1942.

Christmas Day 1942

This is one of the happiest Christmas Days I remember. There was a concert on the ward and the St John Ambulance nurses danced with the patients to a band from the RAF units in the area. Captain Murray served the tinned turkey, handing round cans of cold beer to go with it. I think everyone broke their diet today. Private Watkins, a little the worse for drink, chased Matron Tobin down the steps. Everyone sang songs round the piano – 'Tangerine' appears to be the favourite. When the day staff came off duty at 8pm we were swept off to the RAOC mess at Nursa by jeep, but we were all pretty tired and came back here at midnight after singing carols with the men.

The New Year of 1943 found Mary and me sitting in the garden of Success Villa on our day off looking at the snaps that Corporal Britton had taken of us in the hospital grounds and drinking the tea that Budloo Khan, the bearer, brought. To house the increasing staff there was now a second sisters' bungalow, called Evelyn Lodge. Our hospital was expanding rapidly. We watched the refugees pouring down the Grand Trunk Road once more, just as they had done nine months earlier when driven before the withdrawing British army in their flight from the Japanese. This time they were fleeing from the Japanese bombs which had been dropped on Calcutta during the last month. They did not walk but kept up a steady trot, their pathetic bundles balanced on their heads, calling to each other constantly to make sure no one was left behind. Budloo Khan observed them, stroking his glossy black beard and wagging his turbaned head sagaciously. 'It is the will of Allah,' he said sadly, turning to pick up the tea tray before making his bare-footed way past the areca palms to the kitchen quarters.

By the end of January the convoys coming in by train were becoming larger – sometimes two hundred men at a time – so that more property had to be requisitioned to make room for them. They were still nearly all medical cases, indicating that, unless the wounded were being sent elsewhere, there could not have been much contact with the Japanese in mid-Assam. Then, early in February, we heard that Lady Mary Herbert, the wife of the Governor of Bengal, was coming to pay us a visit. The orderlies plunged into an orgy of 'spit and polish', the sisters chivied the *bhistes* and sweepers and Bunny Austin's patients tried desperately to find pyjamas that were not completely ruined by aniline dyes.

When Lady Mary had visited the hospital in 1942 I had been on night duty so missed seeing her. This time I was on the British medical ward and would escort her round the patients, introducing her to anyone – or anything – noteworthy. Lady Mary was a tall, good-looking brunette in a navy-and-white cloche hat and navy blue coat who took a lively interest in everything she saw. Corporal Dobbs, the only American in my ward, attracted her notice and she listened sympathetically to the heart-rending account he gave her of his diabetes. What neither she nor I knew at the time was that the corporal had smuggled in a chocolate bar, which was even then lying hidden under his pillow ready to be eaten as soon as we had turned our backs. When Lady Mary left us in order to go into conference with Matron Tobin and Mrs Niblock I returned to the ward, in time to catch Corporal Dobbs red-handed scoffing his chocolate bar under the blankets. He was very contrite, promising never to break his dietary rules again, and wrote a letter of apology. I really think the distinguished visitor's interest in his condition caused a change of heart in Corporal Dobbs, for he stopped his candy-smuggling habits and we were able to discharge him shortly afterwards.

Soon after Lady Mary Herbert's visit Matron Tobin called a meeting of sisters in order to break the news that from now on the QAs were to hold commissions in the army with the rank of first lieutenant. She handed round the newly arrived QA reserve medals to those of us who had not received them at Woolwich. At the same time 'pips' were distributed to be attached to our shoulder-flashes, two on each side. This directive was greeted with mixed feelings. The regular sisters in the service had always valued their non-military status as they felt that it made for pleasanter relations with both officers and men. In accepting commissions they feared the loss of that Florence Nightingale image that had endeared them to the British other ranks since the Crimean War. But, as matron reminded us, the situation had become more fluid: 'Tommy Atkins' today could be Lieutenant Thomas Atkins tomorrow. There were opportunities for all in the modern army. We reserve sisters concurred, making the point that, with thousands of women joining the forces and being granted commissions like the men, it would complicate matters if one body of women were out of step.

So we all accepted our changes of status with a good grace though with some regret for a tradition gone for ever. Florence Nightingale had been a member of the original 'Ladies' Committee' which had made arrangements for the training of the first army nurses at Netley, and she continued to keep in touch when the Indian Army Nursing Service was inaugurated in 1883. 'How do you think Miss Nightingale would have reacted to officer sisters?' I asked. 'She would have approved,' said Matron Tobin, lifting Mrs Honey out of her basket and settling down with her on the cane sofa.

Despite the rumours that circulated about Brigadier Wingate's plan to ferry men into the heart of the Burmese jungle and whispers about a mysterious 'V' Force that operated in the Arakan, March brought no change in the type of patients admitted. In fact the numbers began to drop, even long-standing infections recovering in the ideal climatic conditions.

After attending an excellent concert given by the RAF units in the area, where they played every type of music on every type of instrument, we returned to the hospital to find news awaiting us. A Major Ackroyd was coming as second-in-command at the 65th Combined. Teddy was to be commanding officer of a thousand-bed hospital in the forward area. It was to be started from scratch, like Asansol, ready for the large numbers of casualties that were expected in the near future. I presumed that it would mean promotion for Teddy and I was pleased about this. Also I felt that a separation at this stage might be a good thing, miserable as it would be for both of us. I had long ago made up my mind not to commit myself irretrievably to anyone until the war was over and badly needed a breathing space in order to take stock of the situation.

By the time the second season of hot weather approached we sisters had learned quite a few ways to keep cooler. When we first arrived we had darned away at our white art-silk or lisle-thread stockings, knowing that no further supplies were forthcoming, but by now they were past mending and we were reduced to wearing white ankle socks – except for senior regulars who must have hoarded large stocks of hose. We were able to dispense with suspender belts and roll-ons until the cool season, but we always wore cotton slips under the white drill uniforms as the strong sunlight made them transparent. One could leave the two top buttons undone at the neck in very hot weather but three would be considered provocative by some matrons. Bras and panties were always made of pure cotton and were changed at least daily, while uniforms and head-veils might last a whole day if you were lucky. When reports were being written, the forearm that rested on the table sweated so much that a large cotton handkerchief was used as an absorbent pad. Neglect of this precaution could mean an attack of prickly heat. The fashion for rolled-up hair that prevailed in the war years was the best possible style for keeping the head cool, particularly at the back of the neck, where the sweat collected and trickled down the spine. We were better off than the men, who had to wear knee socks, lace-up shoes and often a cap as well.

The hospital was being prepared for the coming heat. Teddy had organised an air-conditioned room of four beds ready for the worst of the heat exhaustions, malarias and skin cases. Bunny Austin could well be deprived of his most interesting patients. The punkahs in the wards and duty rooms were oiled and checked by the electrician and his mate. Everyone was told to take some leave before the flow of sick and fevered men

Lieutenant-Colonel Edward Lossing IMS, 1943.

from jungle and plain changed to a flood in the hot weather.

In May I wrote in my diary:

> Vague stories of Brigadier Wingate's foray into Burma float
> around but it is quite impossible to get at the truth because
> of security. Surely leave would have been postponed if
> anything important was going to happen. What a curious
> business war is; nothing much seems to be happening but
> perhaps we are hearing no news because of security
> regulations. Nobody has actually died – on my ward at least
> – since those tragic heat-exhaustion men. That is something
> to be thankful for.

Miss Tobin, doling out three weeks' leave to all and sundry,
instructed me to take mine as soon as possible. She knew that
it would be the last leave for Teddy before he was posted; she

was also concerned about his health as he had suffered several attacks of fever, which had reduced his already lean frame to an unnatural thinness.

Teddy and I caught the midnight train at the beginning of May, sharing a four-berth compartment with an army captain and sergeant. We lay on the bunks fully-clothed and took turns to use the tiny washroom. Nobody said much as we all wanted to sleep. The journey to Bhim Tal in northern India was to take two days. Early in the morning we slowed down while passing a goods train laden with supplies of grain from the Punjab to alleviate the famine in Bengal, which ultimately killed more than a million people. Creeping along the track under the trucks were dozens of men and woman armed with bits of bamboo, which they pushed up through the slatted floor in order to puncture the sacks of grain. A thin trickle of wheat was their reward, which they caught in small brass bowls. Suddenly the engine's whistle sounded and the train gave a warning lurch. The people scrambled out lest they be trapped by the wheels. I wondered how many parents were maimed or killed in their desperation to obtain food for their families and said so out loud. The sergeant who was standing beside me said that *he* wondered how much grain would be left in the sacks by the time the train reached Calcutta.

We passed through Patna, Allahabad and Lucknow, leaving the train at Bareilly, which we reached at 11 o'clock at night. I slept like a log in the ladies' rest room at the station with two Muslim ladies in purdah while Teddy had a miserable night in a noisy dirty hotel where he was tormented by mosquitoes. On the 5am train to Kathgodam, which was very crowded, an elderly Indian chatted to us all the way, mostly about Gandhi and his 'iniquitous imprisonment'. We told him about the plundering of the goods train. He remarked severely that, because of the Japanese invasion, there was no rice coming in from Burma and asked us when we were going to drive 'those fellows' out of Assam. We were suitably apologetic but explained that we could not manage without Gandhi's cooperation. He demanded to know how the Mahatma could help us when we had put him in jail. This seemed rather a circular argument so we sat and smiled at him. He beamed back expansively through his large spectacles, salaaming affectionately when we left the train. A taxi took us to Bhowali where I was able to buy a light raincoat for the cooler weather in the hills, a green-and-blue check shirt and a pair of blue slacks.

The beautiful secluded lake villages of Bhim Tal and Naini Tal in the foothills of the Himalayas had been a convenient holiday resort for the British in Delhi. The State of Nepal separated the villages from the greater mass of mountains beyond, but these could not be seen from our eyrie, where we were closed in by the slopes above us. From the small hotel, our walks took us past the elegant summer palaces of Indian princes, their façades reflected perfectly in still, stone-edged pools. Not a single dead leaf disturbed the surface of the water and there was no sign of life anywhere.

The hedgerows were thick with wild berries, whose fruit was bright orange in colour when ripe but whose flavour was similar to an English blackberry. They were much appreciated by the children and pack-animals of the wandering hill tribes, who brought their sheep and goats down past the village to graze, heralded by shrill pipes and the tinkling of the bells on their ponies' bridles. They were a picturesque people, the women in brightly-embroidered, long, gathered skirts, with bangles adorning their wrists and coins dangling from their veils. We females eyed each other curiously as I stood with Teddy at the side of the path to let them go by. The children did not beg but lingered to gaze back at us until called sharply by their mothers. In their total absorption in earth and its seasons they reminded me of the gypsies in George Borrow's *Lavengro*.

Lake-fishing was the sport that drew visitors to this isolated spot, for there was plenty of mahseer and hilsa to be caught with the right sort of bait. An ancient fisherman, whose job it was to prepare the rods with a dough-like substance, attended each fishing party; it was with one of these grizzled silent natives that we circumnavigated the lake one morning, finally settling down in a deserted spot to commence a day's sport. He got out the dough, placed it ostentatiously on a stone, then, after looking around in a conspiratorial fashion, dug out a tin of live bait from the mud at his feet, from which he extracted the wriggling creatures that were to be attached to our rods. Naturally we caught some very fine fish, varying from two to eight pounds – the latter the largest for two seasons – but most of them were returned to the water, the rule being that only a limited number of fish could be brought back to the hotel daily. We had no luck fishing from an open boat in the evening, when the lake and its hilly surroundings were far too beautiful for strict concentration, and a pair of wild ducks cavorting above our heads distracted our attention with their desolate cries.

During our last long walk at Bhim Tal, Teddy and I came to a clearing surrounded by a few slender trees. Here, where the dappled light filtered through the leaves, on a branch six feet from the ground, perched a tiny nest on which a bird was sitting. It took no notice of us and we were able to examine it minutely. Its head and neck were a glossy midnight blue, the back grey merging into a white front and the wings chestnut. The tail feathers formed two silvery streamers which hung down, almost a foot long, from the nest. We stood entranced.

After a while it flew off, floating dreamily through the grove catching insects on the wing, its long tail feathers rising and falling like spun-glass ribbons. It was a male paradise flycatcher, a summer visitor from the Middle East.

When the bird disappeared into the trees I crept forward, gently reached up and drew the branch towards me so that I could look into the nest. One pink egg with tan-coloured freckles lay there, breathtaking in its perfection. A sense of wonder and awe swept over me. Then disaster struck. The twig I was holding broke off and the released branch shot into the air, projecting the egg up high, round in an arc and down to earth, smashing it into nothingness.

I was inconsolable. In vain did Teddy tell me that the flycatcher's mate would lay another egg; something exquisite had been destroyed – and by my hand. The light went out of the day and we walked despondently back to the hotel.

Like many places in India, Bhim Tal had its scourge in the form of infective hepatitis, which I had the misfortune to catch at the end of the holiday. I became very ill and as the nearest hospital was at Ranikhet some miles away I had to face a very unpleasant journey. Four hill porters carried me in a *dandy* – a sling of canvas cloth attached to bamboo poles – to a valley where an ambulance was waiting for me on the road. The irregular motion of the *dandy* on the rough terrain increased the intense and miserable nausea which is the worst symptom of the disease. How I would have enjoyed that fascinating descent in different circumstances. Once we reached the road the worst was over and within an hour I was in a private room in the British military hospital being looked after by one of our own QA sisters.

At this point Teddy had to leave me to return to duty at Asansol but I was too ill to care. After a few days on a starvation allowance of heavily diluted lime juice and raw tomatoes,

'George the Commando' and the author at Naini Tal, June 1943.

which was my colleague's interpretation of a fat-free diet, I was very weak indeed – too weak even to wash myself. I asked the sister if I might have a blanket bath, to which she consented with an ill grace, sending in an Indian ayah who washed me in a quiet, soothing way, no doubt removing impurities from the skin brought about by the presence of bile in the circulation. I started to feel better immediately and asked for something to eat.

In a day or two I was able to sit up for the first time to comb my hair, startled to see in the mirror a thin-faced, lemon-skinned apparition. I hurriedly put down the mirror and looked towards the window.

The great range of the Himalaya mountains stretched along the horizon, rosy-pink in the early morning. Day after day I lay propped up with pillows, drinking in strength and peace from those distant snows, thinking that all the suffering and misery of jaundice was worth undergoing for one glimpse of that sublime grandeur.

As soon as I was able I took out my neglected diary and wrote:

It has been a salutary experience to have been at the receiving end of nursing care. It's not what is done to you that matters but the attitude of the one who does it. To be utterly helpless and totally dependent on others was something I knew nothing about. To feel like a helpless child again when you are ill is not unpleasant but to be completely at the mercy of other people's moods and regulations – there's the rub. Now I know what it feels like and I hope it will make me a better nurse.

After a medical board had been held I was told that I could not return to the plains until the monsoons broke and was sent to nearby Naini Tal. In a week or two I was able to join in the social round of the community, which consisted of English and White Russian residents and a few convalescents from hospitals on the plains. I met George the Commando, who wore a large, floppy, khaki hat and was much in demand because of his magnificent tenor voice. He did not say where he came from and I didn't ask. He was the only commando I ever met in India.

Teddy wrote to say that Majors Ackroyd and Austin had been posted elsewhere and that he himself had infective hepatitis. I was appalled. Jaundice down on the plains would destroy any good his holiday had done him. Club residents told me that Bhim Tal Hotel was notorious for jaundice and that many guests developed it when they returned home.

By now I had almost regained the stone in weight that I had lost. As the rains had arrived in Bengal, I was allowed to return to Asansol. I had been away for nearly eight weeks. On the Lucknow train a young officer told me that Orde Wingate's

77th Indian Infantry Brigade had crossed the Chindwin River in northern Burma and disrupted the railway between Myitkyina and Mandalay. Something was being done to dislodge the Japanese from Burma after all but at the cost of many lives.

Teddy took a long time to recover from the jaundice. His weight went down alarmingly but by August he was almost his old self. We heard that Lord Mountbatten was to take command in South East Asia and that an American was to be his second-in-command, but that was all. The cool weather would surely be the signal for some sort of campaign. In the meantime we would continue to cope with the diseases of India, with the flies, with the mosquitoes and with the daily grind in the hothouse atmosphere.

In the middle of September the news of my posting to Gauhati came through. I was not surprised: a year-and-a-half was a long time to be left in the same place, one had to be philosophical about it. I could not imagine what it would be like not to see Teddy each day and wondered where he would be posted to when he left Asansol at the end of the month.

On my last evening, when I had finished packing, I wandered round the compound of Success Villa, taking leave of my first little corner of the real India. Outside my window the banana tree that the monkeys had stripped of fruit one summer night stood like a pale uncouth ghost in the dusk. The broad leaves of the areca palms showed black against the sky. From their roosting tree the restless egrets murmured and stretched their wings before settling for the night. The only other sound came from the bullfrogs round the distant tank. As I turned to go indoors, a late rickshaw passed along the Grand Trunk Road, its faint lamp swaying, the soft insistent 'tonk, tonk,' of its bell tolling the knell on a chapter of my life that had gone for ever.

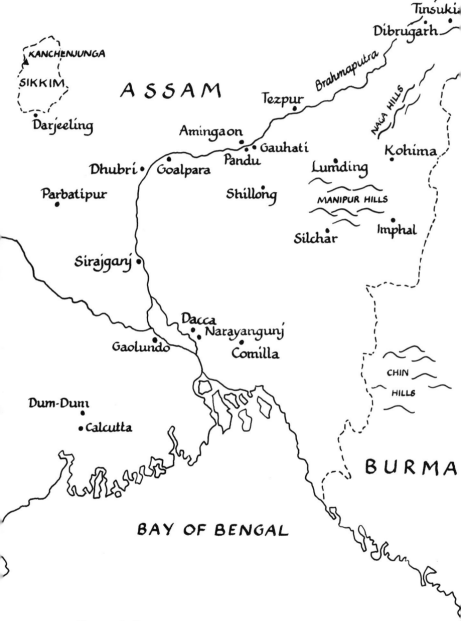

Eastern India

4 · Enemy at the Gates

Seated in the corner of a two-berth sleeper of the Darjeeling mail train on the way to Gauhati, with the darkness spreading over the slums of Calcutta, a sense of isolation and depression swept through me and I burst into a torrent of tears, to the consternation of the middle-aged Jewish woman who shared the compartment with me. Asansol had become my home, the abode of the first person I had truly loved and who had loved me in return. Now I was destined to travel, friendless and alone, to a new life in a strange country called Assam, six hundred miles away. I was very sorry for myself.

Comforted by my kindly travelling companion, who was on her way to meet her husband in Darjeeling, I wiped my eyes, blew my nose and unpacked my map of India to follow the route to my destination. I saw that Gauhati stood on the south bank of the Brahmaputra where it ran level with the Himalayan foothills. After a tiring journey lasting a day and a night I alighted at the railhead of Amingaon to embark on a ferry steamer that drifted slowly across the river to Pandu. It was seven o'clock in the evening when I reached Temple Ghat, where I had a three-hour wait in the gathering dusk before an ambulance arrived from Gauhati to take me to the 52nd Indian General Hospital (C). The 'C' meant that British troops were catered for as well as Indians. Before long such hospitals were generally known as Combined Military Hospitals.

In the sisters' mess the matron took one look at me and gave me the following day off. There had been no food on the train and I had not been able to sleep. I caught a glimpse of the hospital through the trees, sat down to a meal that I was too weary to eat and was eventually carried by ambulance to the Upper Bungalow well over a mile away where some of the sisters lived.

Twelve hours later I woke from a refreshing sleep to find

myself lying on a camp bed in a room full of sunshine. A sister sat at the plain, deal, army-supply table filing her nails. To my surprise it was Mary King, the beautiful reserved girl I had last encountered in Calcutta. 'I thought you would never wake up,' she said. 'Doris Oliver and Isobel McKenzie are waiting to see you.'

I jumped out of bed, sliding my feet into my *chapplis* and swinging the unsuitable blue wool dressing-gown that I had brought from England over my shoulders. In the next room I found Isobel McKenzie looking just as sturdy as ever, but Doris had lost weight since the *Monarch of Bermuda* days and she showed me the two extra holes she had cut in her belt in order to make it fit. The expression in her peat-brown eyes, self-mocking and worldly-wise, remained as I remembered it. The warm welcome cheered me up and I unpacked my canvas wash-basin and rope-handled pail almost jauntily. Once more I was back to camping conditions – cold tap dripping over a tin hip-bath and wooden commodes in the bathrooms.

An ambulance arrived to take us to the sisters' mess in the hospital compound for lunch, where I glanced round the dining table with astonishment. How, I asked myself, did such a bevy of fair-skinned, golden-haired beauties come together in the backwoods of Assam? There was Marty Adair from Belfast, whose fiancé, Doris told me, was fighting in Assam with the Royal Artillery, Monica Lamb from the Home Counties, Marjorie Pringle from the north of England, Joan Inman (the only brunette) from London and several others, whom I had not seen since we arrived in India. The sun had lightened English 'mouse' hair to a soft gold and changed milk-and-roses complexions to peaches and cream. I thought there must be a male connoisseur of female pulchritude in league with Matron Summerfield, collecting a harem of lovelies for his delectation. Perhaps the commanding officer!

On my allotted ward of British patients next morning I wrestled with the diet sheets, which, as usual, defeated me. I left the duty room in search of advice. Seeing a man working at a table in what appeared to be an office, I burst in unceremoniously saying, 'Can you help me, please?' He was most cooperative, studying the sheets with interest. After a while he scratched his head and spoke on the telephone to the quartermaster.

While he was talking I had a good look at him. He was middle-aged, tall and loose-limbed with head thrust forward

The passenger ferry over the Brahmaputra at Pandu, 1945.

as though his pugilistic shoulders prevented him from standing upright. He had a decidedly pugnacious chin: I would not have liked to cross swords – or words – with him. On his desk was a wide-brimmed bush hat. I very nearly asked what his job was but suddenly noticed the full colonel's insignia on his shoulder-tabs. The quartermaster bustled in, a sheaf of army forms clipped to a board under his arm, his ruddy face glowing even though the weather was moderately cool. 'Sister is having trouble with army form AFN 734,' said the colonel. 'See if you can help, quartermaster.'

I thanked the colonel and followed the tubby little QM out of the office and into my duty room. Eventually the expert helped me to get the measure of the subsistence and other diets for the time being at least, then leaned forward confidingly, 'Do you realise who that man in the office is, sister?' he said in a hushed voice. 'Colonel Cawthorn, the commanding officer of this hospital!' 'Definitely not the "harem" type,' I thought to myself, absolving the colonel from all complicity in the matter of the beautiful blondes.

Soon after I arrived the weather changed for the worse. The rain bucketed down relentlessly, causing a sea of mud to suck and squelch round our Wellington boots as we crossed from mess to ward. I understood why concrete paths had been built to join the rows of wards to the administrative buildings; anything on wheels would otherwise have become bogged down, particularly trolley stretchers. The wood and bamboo *bashas*, which held up to forty patients, remained surprisingly dry and airy, chiefly because they were constructed with a gap between the roof and the walls, and with eaves that extended a long way out to cast a shadow and disperse rain drippings. Some of the floors were of dried mud, others covered with woven matting; functional electric light bulbs hanging from the rafters and electrically-powered punkahs gave erratic witness to the presence of the twentieth century. At the end of the ward was the sweeper's domain, where he came and went with his large basketwork container with close-fitting lid which kept the bedpans safe from flies. But the *bhiste* made no concession to the modern world whatever. In dry weather he squatted in the sandy dust, scouring the tin plates and utensils with the earth around him before rinsing them scrupulously clean with water from a brass bowl.

Sometimes I got lost, as all the rows of hutments looked alike, but after a week I learned to count the *bashas* in both directions in order to pinpoint my ward and from then on I had no problems.

28 September 1943

This is a red-letter day for the nursing staff. We have all been issued with two suits of khaki drill – bush shirts and trousers – to be worn from 6pm on as a protection against mosquitoes. There was a good deal of commotion and unrestrained merriment at the Upper Bungalow as we tried on our trousers, which were too long and too loose, and the shirts, which were on the tight side. Women seem to come in more shapes and sizes than men. After the application of a little tailoring skill we all managed to make ourselves look respectable, if not dashing.

I believe we wore khaki for the first time when we attended Colonel Ackroyd's lectures on 'Diet for the Patients' in the evening. He had what we thought was a bee in his bonnet about

QAIMNS sisters in khaki. Left to right: Isobel McKenzie, the author, Doris Oliver, Marty Adair and an unidentified nurse at their bungalow, Gauhati, Assam, 1943.

the therapeutic value of yoghurt – or rather the Indian form of it, which was made of buffalo milk and had heavy white curds. I used to notice that every day the cooks brought round to the wards great shallow metal containers, one holding beautiful fried fish, the other something that looked like the curds that are produced when rennet is added to warm fresh milk, familiar to me since my childhood. Colonel Ackroyd, who had been at Asansol for a short time and who was now second-in-command at Gauhati, was convinced that convalescents and those with digestive disturbances who were unwilling eaters would benefit markedly from having curds introduced into their diet. There were pro-curd and anti-curd factions but I think the persistent colonel may have been right: yoghurt has been found to have many remarkable properties.

Captain Grodd, a portly Jewish doctor from South Africa with whom I worked, took me along to a social gathering at the RAMC mess to meet other members of the medical staff. There I was introduced to the enormously tall, broad-shouldered Captain Patterson; Captain Bennett-Jones, a young

North Welshman with a smooth, rosy complexion; Colonel Ransome,[1] the medical specialist; and Major Niblock, who bore the same name as the civil surgeon at Asansol.

Representatives from 202 Area Headquarters were present, some of them entertainment officers who were looking for local talent. They immediately descended on the QAs, requesting volunteers for a revue at the Garrison Theatre to be put on as a diversion for the patients and staff at the hospital. Joan Inman, the petite, curly-haired girl I had noticed at the sisters' mess, Marjorie Pringle, who had taken part in the concert on the *Monarch of Bermuda*, and I agreed to help them out. We also promised to find some Red Cross and St John Ambulance nurses to join us.

We started right away, meeting three times a week after we came off duty, but when it was discovered that the rehearsals were to last until midnight there was a rebellion. We could not possibly work all day and rehearse half the night. It was not fair to us, nor was it fair to our patients, in whose interests the revue was meant to be. While we were pleading for shorter rehearsals something happened which drove all thoughts of entertainment out of our heads.

Colonel Cawthorn had decided that the RAMC mess should hold a buffet party with dancing in the only *basha* with a suitable floor – a set of joined planks which were liberally sprinkled with talcum powder. It was a rare occasion. The men were to wear mess dress and the sisters were asked to wear evening frocks if they had them. Out came my black and silver dress made from a sari. I didn't like it much; it was too *femme fatale* for me but no doubt the men would appreciate it.

My diary continues the tale:

On Saturday 23 October 1943 a terrible thing happened. The RAMC dance had started and the revelry was at its height with everyone dancing when I noticed that one of the pictures on the wall was swinging from side to side. I drew my partner's attention to it but he merely laughed and said that someone must have put too much pineapple juice in the punch. Suddenly a voice shouted – I think it was Colonel Cawthorn's – 'Everybody outside quickly. Hurry! Hurry!' and we all dashed out into the pitch-black night

---

[1] Later Sir Gordon Ransome, Professor Emeritus of Medicine, University of Singapore, 1972–1978.

leaving the gramophone playing away eerily in the deserted room. As we stumbled over tree roots the ground beneath our feet oscillated backwards and forwards and then up and down. We all subsided on to the ground willy-nilly listening to the low grumbling of the disturbed earth. After about three minutes from the start of it (which seemed like a lifetime) the tremor ceased.

I am writing this in the early hours as I can't sleep thinking about the earthquake and hoping there won't be any more tremors. Whatever else moves, you expect the ground under your feet to be solid, reliable, the one certainty you can depend on. The horror of that moment when there seems to be no safety anywhere shakes you to the core. No one panicked but perhaps the drinks they had had at the party gave them Dutch courage.

The next day we heard that a crack had appeared in the earth under a village further north, causing the death of several peasants who had disappeared down it. The last earthquake, the worst known in India, had taken place in North Bihar in 1934. In our area of Assam, the town of Shillong sixty miles away was devastated in 1897.

In a chastened mood we returned to our rehearsals, putting on the revue less than a week after the earthquake, despite the fact that we were far from ready. How such a poorly-rehearsed mixed bag of antics turned out so well I cannot imagine, but it wasn't at all bad. The most applauded act was a mime by a demure-looking Eurasian girl in a long flowing frock, who drifted on to the stage while a choir sang soulfully:

'She was such a shy maiden, her looks were downcast,
With an innocent air like a maid from the past.'

Verse after verse continued while the maiden floated about gracefully and the audience got itself into a thoroughly romantic mood. She must have been the epitome of all that the men were dreaming of, for from my place in the wings I noticed that there was a certain amount of surreptitious nose-blowing going on in the darkened theatre. At the last line of the last verse the music quickened and the voices sang:

'What a naughty young lady she was round behind.'

The dancer turned her back to the audience, revealing scarlet panties and a costume that ended at the waistline. The soldiers stamped their feet and cheered, no doubt considering it delightfully shocking, which it was at that time and place.

While we had been missing out on sleep because of rehearsals, the other QAs in the mess had been having problems of their own. The rats were getting above themselves: they were actually trying to gnaw the sisters' elbows and toes through the mosquito nets. We suspected that the repulsive rodents were after the citronella with which we were supposed to anoint our exposed skin areas to discourage mosquitoes. We hated the revolting greasy salve with its unpleasant odour which made the skin smart and the eyes burn if it accidentally got into them. The old soldiers declared that the citronella was left over from the Great War and I expect they were right. It was not nearly so efficient as the lotion the American servicemen were issued with, which was superior in every way, being odourless, colourless and astringent. We swapped our drink ration for bottles of the American mosquito repellent, which made for satisfaction all round.

The sisters got together to complain to Miss Summerfield about the rats. An Indian rat-catcher was called in, who lured them away from the mess by laying a trail of poisoned bait. However, we attributed their continued absence to our veto on citronella.

Colonel Ransome, the medical specialist, sported a handlebar moustache and was very advanced in his thinking. It was he who arranged for us to be taught how to give intravenous injections at a time when many of the British doctors were being drafted to the forward areas to be replaced by Indians. The technique was very different from the ordinary hypodermic injection routine which we had carried out from our second-year training days, practising on oranges and then on each other. Not only were there risks involved for the beginner, but in certain patients it was quite difficult to get a needle into the vein at all. I always hoped that there would never be an occasion when I would feel it my duty to give an injection of intravenous quinine.

The colonel kept a very close eye on the medical wards under his jurisdiction, making sure that every patient received his anti-malarial mepacrine by demanding that a square on his chart should be coloured yellow by the sisters after each dose. Not that it made much difference on the Indian wards, for we used to find little hoards of pills on the wooden ledges between the roof of the *bashas* and the walls which had been put there by patients who thought they would cause sterility.

Every week the CO, who was an Australian, carried out a ward inspection with the quartermaster and the subahdar-major, Anzac hat pulled well down on his head, his boxer's shoulders hunched and his officer's cane used as an extension of his hand as he probed into corners and lifted the towel from the sterile medication tray. Medical officers and sisters shook in their shoes when Colonel Cawthorn started his rounds and mopped their brows when he moved on to the next ward, jabbing his cane eloquently in the air as he harangued the quartermaster. The standards he set were very high and as a result the hospital ran as near to clockwork as ever an Indian hospital could.

In the Upper Bungalow the atmosphere was very different. The servants, who lived in huts surrounded by banana trees at the end of the compound, were the most primitive Indians we had come across, recruited as they were from hamlets deep in the Bengal jungle. They were unable to speak either English or the language of the locals in the Gauhati bazaar.

Their duties were not onerous: they boiled up the water for baths in large kerosine tins, carrying it up to the house in pails; they cleaned the rooms – or rather moved the dust around with a bunch of twigs and grasses; and they cut the lawn with a pair of scissors borrowed from Mary King's sewing box. No matter how much equipment we begged from the quartermaster for them, it always evaporated like morning dew in the direction of the village bric-à-brac booth.

One day my framed print of a golden-haired child with red ribbons in her hair, by Renoir, disappeared from the bedroom wall. It had been given to me by an artist friend just before I left England and I valued it greatly. Nobody could understand what had happened to it; one could hardly blame the rats, cunning though they were. As the weeks went by and no explanation for the picture's removal presented itself, I gave it up for lost; so many things disappeared without trace in that poverty-stricken land.

A few weeks before Christmas, Marty Adair had occasion to go to the end of the compound in order to find out why the hot water for the evening baths had not arrived. The place was deserted apart from a six-year-old child, who pointed towards the bazaar and said '*Puja*', meaning that there was a

In the garden of the Upper Bungalow, Gauhati: QAIMNS sisters Doris Oliver and Marty Adair.

festival going on. Marty peered into one of the empty huts, the walls of which were covered in coloured prints of Hindu gods and goddesses. In the centre, occupying the place of honour, was my missing Renoir. I did not have the heart to demand its return. Perhaps even to this day, in some village temple deep in Bengal, a little Parisienne reigns supreme among the picture-pantheon of Hindu gods.

Late in October Bennett-Jones took over from Sandy Grodd on my ward. I enjoyed working with him as he had exactly the right balance of professionalism and friendliness in his manner towards me. The British patients appreciated him too as a man they could discuss their worries with.

'BJ' was still in his twenties, fresh-faced and fair-complexioned, with a rather hesitant air. He used to sidle into the duty room with an anxious expression in his slightly prominent hazel eyes as though anticipating a problem which would be beyond his competence to solve. The sola topi he wore for his morning ward round proclaimed his newness to India; in the evening he favoured a jaunty forage cap and shining Sam

Browne, which invested him with an aura of supreme confidence. He would settle down in the duty room with a cup of tea to discuss any interesting cases on the ward. In the distance the jackals kept up a wolf-like howling above which could be heard the occasional scream of a hyena.

The British convalescents sat outside talking to the Indian orderlies while the *bhiste* and sweeper stood respectfully in the background, waiting for any crumbs of conversation that might be tossed their way. Our soldiers picked up Urdu expressions quickly enough, using them fairly indiscriminately to try to make themselves understood. Sometimes their efforts led to a gross lack of comprehension, particularly when the patients used what they believed to be Urdu words but which the Indians presumed were English. The various accents of the British Isles could turn a simple request for *garam pani* (hot water) into a puzzle for the purist. I once heard the *bhiste* telling the soldiers how he set about cooking a certain rice dish: 'We put in hot water, same as your English gurumparnee,' he declared, much to the mystification of his audience.

The other group of Indians we had dealings with were the havildars of the Indian Army, who spoke just enough English to produce the sort of comic situations that are used to good effect in television programmes about wartime India. One day I had occasion to ring the transport office in Gauhati and, after stating my name and business, asked, 'Who is that speaking?' 'It is myself,' came the confident rejoinder.

Though many problems arose through misunderstandings between the Indians and ourselves, I once had to cope with a situation that I understood only too well. There was a certain orderly named Hari Lal who was always asleep with his head resting on the ward table when I did my midnight round of the Indian blocks. I felt sorry for him because I knew how desperate the need for sleep could be, but he was breaking a very strict rule in neglecting his patients. After three nights of fruitless remonstration I decided to go for advice to the subahdar-major, who was a person of some importance, being Colonel Cawthorn's right-hand man in all matters concerning the Indian sepoys who worked as orderlies or ambulance drivers.

This subahdar-major had grown old in the service of the British army. He was very broad and bearded, his stomach a monument to the mountains of rice he had demolished over the years. His large khaki turban, like those of the taxi drivers of Chrowringhee, spread itself in an unwieldy shape above his grizzled face. On his chest a row of service medals from many campaigns clinked together, giving warning of his presence to many a military malefactor. In the past he had never failed to calm my exasperation with his wise advice and I had always come away wondering what I had been making a fuss about. This time, however, he put on a stern expression. 'He is a *bad-mash* [villain] and needs teaching a lesson; please to send him to me, sister sahib.' He stood to attention, though his stomach did not, and saluted.

The following night Hari Lal was asleep as usual. I had been thinking during the day what to do about him as I knew how severe would be the punishment meted out to him by the subahdar-major. I asked one of the malaria patients to lend me his pyjama cord. He obliged, watching with curiosity as I tied it round the pile of twenty-four brass ashtrays on the ward table. Then I looped the cord over the sleeper's head. 'Hari Lal!' I called out in a loud voice. He shot into the air and the ashtrays crashed about his ears, to the accompaniment of a crescendo of laughter from his long-suffering patients. After that I had no more trouble from Hari Lal. He became an exemplary orderly.

One night I found a batch of letters from Teddy waiting for me. He had been moving about India, working at hospitals in Bombay, Calcutta and Lucknow, and picking up dengue fever in the process. Now he was needed to establish a hospital almost from scratch, as at Asansol. It was to be the 124th Indian General Hospital at Silchar in the Manipur area, fifty miles as the crow flies from Imphal. What interested me was that it was a mere 120 miles from Gauhati with only the Shillong plateau in between. His appointment at Silchar started on New Year's Day and he wanted me to meet him in Shillong for a couple of days beforehand.

Miss Summerfield willingly gave permission, as it was the custom for a sister to be granted a day off for each week she had been on night duty. Taking into consideration that I would be missing all the Christmas celebrations this year, she allowed me three days in Shillong.

The 52nd Indian General Hospital laid on the customary festivities for the patients at Christmas 1943, but I had no part in them, sleeping soundly all through Christmas Day. When I finished night duty at the end of December, Dorothy Baker, a senior Australian sister who had recently arrived, travelled with me to Shillong. We made the long tortuous ascent in a jeep driven by a REME captain universally known as 'Recovery Joe'. The road was steep and narrow with deep precipices on either side which were strewn with the battered bodies of vehicles that had gone over the edge. Because there was no room to pass, the traffic took turns in having right of way: three hours up and three hours down. Patients in ambulances going up to the plateau to convalesce frequently became car-sick, arriving at the hospital in a state of collapse.

Shillong was the nearest leave station at any altitude south of Gauhati. Perched on an outcrop of rocky plateau land tethered to the Chin and Manipur Hills, it towered above the Assam plain like a fortified town, with fine views in several directions. On the southern side lay Cherrapunji, which boasted an average annual rainfall of 550 inches, the heaviest in the world. The south-west monsoons shed their rain in the amphitheatre of the escarpment on that side, but Shillong itself had an ideal climate, as soft and mild as an English summer.

'Recovery Joe' dropped Dorothy and me at the Women's Auxiliary Corps hostel, where Teddy was waiting, looking his usual lean tanned self. Later, in the unaccustomed opulence of the Pinewood Hotel, we sat by a blazing fire whose pine logs distilled a sweet incense, reinforcing the atmosphere of an English country club evoked by the Findlater's sherry we were sipping. It was bliss to see Teddy again after three months' separation and we – or rather I – talked non-stop through a dinner which I counted as my Christmas celebration.

It wasn't long before we reached the subject of his new hospital. I asked him whether he wouldn't be dangerously placed if the Japanese infiltrated the Manipur area. He responded by asking me whether I had heard of General Slim, who was commander-in-chief of the new Fourteenth Army. I said I hadn't and wanted to know what the general was going to do. 'Set the East ablaze,' he said playfully and would say no more.

In the morning we went shopping; Teddy bought a fine bow to shoot the pigeons which he had learned were becoming a menace at his new hospital. There were diversions for everyone in Shillong: riding, fishing and shooting for the energetic; and for the weary, gentle walks to view the terraces of orange and lemon trees with their dark, glossy leaves. In the evening we found a cinema, where we watched Greer Garson in *Random Harvest* agonising over Ronald Colman as the hero who lost his memory.

Medical staff, 52nd General Hospital, Gauhati, 1944. Second row: fifth from left, Lieutenant-Colonel Ransome RAMC; seventh from left, Colonel F R Cawthorn IMS; Colonel J A Crawford RAMC; the Subhadar-Major.
Third row: seventh from left, Lieutenant Jones (Quartermaster); ninth from left, Captain Sandy Grodd RAMC. Back row: extreme right, Captain N Bennett-Jones RAMC.

On the final day of our stay in Shillong, Dorothy Baker and her friend Clem met Teddy and me at the Assam Industries Centre, where we bought warm skirts and stockings for the colder weather in the New Year. Outside the gates of a large bungalow close by we watched an animal tamer holding a pole with a tray attached on which were two tiny monkeys. They were dressed in tawdry scraps of male and female clothing and were made to dance and perform acrobatic feats, being prodded by their owner if they slowed down. Sadder still was the plight of a young black bear with a muzzle of woven cane over his snout, who was made to sway backwards and forwards rhythmically to the music of a drum. These itinerant Assamese showmen appeared to be the equivalent of the Bengal snakecharmers, providing entertainment for the villagers and a living for themselves.

Shillong is a trysting place for separated couples: wives and husbands; engaged pairs; star-crossed lovers. How their ghosts must haunt its pine-clad slopes. Here in Gauhati Colonel Cawthorn's wife has come to stay until 12 January. By all accounts she is a charming person. The CO looks cheerful and swings his cane about in a jaunty fashion. The RAMC have put on a New Year party for her tonight.

Hardly had Mrs Cawthorn departed to continue her war work elsewhere in India than Captain Bennett-Jones and I found that we had a crisis on our hands. In our side ward we had two identically ill pioneer corps Indians isolated, with very high fevers but no malarial parasites in their blood. They complained of severe frontal headache and difficulty in breathing. There was no rash of any kind. We watched their condition deteriorating day by day while BJ burned the midnight oil in search of a diagnosis in his tropical medicine books. He called in Colonel Ransome, who read the case papers and viewed the patients, twiddling his pointed moustachios in perplexity. Colonel Ransome sought advice from his Indian colleagues but the only senior one in the hospital was Captain Qerishi, the surgeon, who was not an expert on medical ailments.

Two days later, after bleeding from nose and mouth, both patients died. An elderly Indian doctor gave his opinion that the men had contracted an internal type of smallpox which affected the mucous membrane instead of the skin and which, he declared, was always fatal.

Captain Bennett-Jones and I looked at each other aghast, both silently calculating the date of our last vaccination. It was over two years before! We were far from happy, knowing that sporadic cases of smallpox occurred even in those who had been vaccinated. Hurriedly we collected together the various orderlies, *bhistes* and sweepers who had been in contact with the victims and led them off to the laboratory to be vaccinated with us. We knew that we had a very unpleasant two weeks ahead of us. When the quarantine period was over and nobody in our group had developed the disease, BJ brought along an old medical dictionary he had found. It stated: 'In "Malignant Smallpox", fortunately rare, the patient may die from excessive doses of the toxin, prior to the stage of eruption of the rash.' We solemnly shook hands, giving thanks for our deliverance

126

and that of all our staff.

After two months on the Indian psychiatric wards, where I felt particularly useless and ignorant, I went to Matron Summerfield and asked for a change of duty. Having just recovered from another attack of dengue fever I was very low in health and spirits. Miss Summerfield, kindly but colourless, advised me to take cod-liver oil and malt, but then she suddenly perked up and said that she had the very thing for me: a hospital river steamer was just about to leave on a short trip to Sirajganj with a complement of patients for the 67th Combined Military Hospital. Colonel Cameron from our hospital, who had a full-length plaster on his broken leg, would be on the ship too and I could keep a special watch on him. I accepted with alacrity for I had heard conflicting reports about what it was like on the river and wanted to see for myself.

1 March 1944

I love being on the river. Our steamer is called the *Mikir* and we have about sixty Indians on board plus Colonel Cameron, who appears to be quite comfortable sitting on deck with his huge plaster resting on a stool. My assistant is a quiet, attractive-looking Anglo-Indian girl called Nurse Piggott and the doctor is in the Indian Army Medical Corps. The meals leave a lot to be desired, consisting of goat stew or chicken curry, but maybe I could coax the cook into producing a mixed grill of some sort. After two days' sailing, we handed our patients over to the RTO at Sirajganj, though I don't know if the initials stand for Regional Transport Officer or River Transport Officer.

On the homeward journey the master of the vessel invited the medical and nursing staff (all three of us) to his eyrie above the top deck to survey the passing countryside. He indicated the direction of the Naga Hills, remarking that a 'Miss sahib' lived there. I was taken aback and asked 'British Miss sahib?' 'British lady, yes,' said the master, wagging his head from side to side; and that was all I could get out of him.

It was not until the war was long over that I discovered the identity of the mysterious 'Miss sahib'. I picked up a book in Blackwell's of Oxford entitled *Naga Paths* by Ursula Graham-Bower. She had visited India when she was twenty-three and had fallen in love with the Naga Hills, where the warrior inhabitants had almost given up their head-hunting habits. Two years later she returned as photographer and anthropologist, being treated by some of the Nagas as the reincarnation of a much-loved chieftainess. When the Japanese began to encroach on Imphal and Kohima in March 1944 she organised her tribesmen into reconnaissance bands to spy for the British. They rounded up escaped prisoners, deserters and refugees from the battle area. Miss Graham-Bower's Nagas apprehended these people with the aid of rather antiquated flintlock rifles and put them on the train for Gauhati. This 'Naga Queen', who married an English colonel at the end of the war, was one more in the long line of Englishwomen (or, in her case, Scotswomen) who set out for a foreign land, felt a kinship for its people and acted as leader, mentor and friend.

Back at Gauhati there was a feeling of excitement in the air because a Fourteenth Army general had visited the hospital on 9 March to talk to Colonel Cawthorn. Nobody seemed to know who he was but I wondered whether it was General Slim himself.

Shortly after my return Colonel Cawthorn called all the RAMC personnel and those sisters who could be spared to a briefing on the part the hospital would play in the campaign that was to take place in Assam. After first aid treatment in a field ambulance depot or casualty clearing station, the wounded would be flown out to hospitals at Tezpur, Panitola, Dibrugarh, Comilla, Silchar and Gauhati. They would then be moved on by river steamer, train and air to military hospitals in India to make room for the next convoy of wounded.

The colonel put us 'in the picture' with regard to the position of Gauhati in the conflict. The Gauhati area was the bottle-neck between mid-Assam and India and therefore strategically vulnerable. There were two approaches for the enemy: both led through Manipur state to Gauhati, one by road via Silchar and Shillong, the other by rail from Manipur Road. From Gauhati the enemy had only to cross the Brahmaputra and they would be on the road to New Delhi.

General Slim wanted us to know what was involved in the struggle so that we could give him all the help we possibly could. Unless the fighting men could be kept fit or returned to battle quickly the campaign would be put in jeopardy.

It was a moving appeal and we responded. Nobody took leave although it wasn't actually cancelled for another month. We heard that fifty sisters could be arriving from the forward area at any time. The rumours circulating were depressing ones. Matron told us that, because the Japanese treated women prisoners so badly, it was the policy of the army not to risk leaving them in areas that could be overrun by the enemy, though we all knew that QA sisters were attached to forward medical units.

On 30 March Teddy rang from Silchar to tell me that General Wingate had been killed but asked me not to say anything until the event was made public. A week later the principal QA matron in the area, Miss Loughnan, visited us to confer with Miss Summerfield, who afterwards broke the news that Marty Adair's fiancé, Geoffrey, had been killed near Kohima.

8 April 1944

Today a mobile hospital, the 66th Indian General, complete with nineteen QA sisters, arrived from Manipur Road. They came by train, as they were at the next but one railway stop to us, and had a most uncomfortable journey. We begged for news, but all they could tell us was that they were evacuated because the Japanese were making for Kohima and Imphal. This is not good. Teddy wrote to say all was well but his letter is several days old. He has to go up to Shillong to see somebody of importance at the hospital on 14 April and wonders if there is any chance at all that we could see each other that day. I'll ask matron but it's most unlikely she will let me go.

I did ask Miss Summerfield and, wonder of wonders, she happened to be looking for someone to take four patients up to Shillong by ambulance. But when we started up those terrifying slopes with a rather swashbuckling Sikh driver at the wheel, whom I suspected of showing off, I began to regret it. Halfway up the driver had to turn round in his own space when an army truck in front stopped suddenly, leaving us momentarily suspended with two wheels over nothingness. I shut my eyes and prayed. When I opened them again we were on the road, with the Sikh a pale shade of grey and with sounds of vomiting coming from the convalescents at the back of the ambulance. Whatever happened I was determined not to return with that particular driver and his vehicle.

After leaving my pallid patients at the hospital I went to the club, where Teddy arrived within half-an-hour. Over lunch we discussed our own affairs but afterwards we went for a walk in the pine woods and he told me about General Wingate. His Mitchell bomber, Teddy said, had come down in the Manipur Hills on the evening of 24 March. By the time a search party had been organised from Silchar, with doctors from the hospital joining in the two-day climb, all that was found in the area of the crash was the wreckage of the aircraft, dead and burned bodies and Orde Wingate's sun helmet, which symbolised him as much as the cigar symbolised Winston Churchill, his greatest admirer. Teddy took charge of the charred and battered topi, but I never learned its subsequent history.

Teddy explained the part the Chindits were playing in the present campaign, telling me that at the beginning of March General Wingate's second expedition of long-range penetration troops had been ferried by glider into Burma, where they were totally dependent on airborne supplies. They were there to support the American General Stilwell in the north and General Slim in the centre. Orde Wingate's death was not made public immediately in case it had a depressing effect on his brigades at a very critical time in the campaign. During the afternoon I handed over the knee socks I had knitted for Teddy on night duty and took the regular carrier service back to Gauhati.

On 25 April, after being with us for seventeen days, the sisters from the 66th Indian General Hospital packed up to return to Manipur Road. It seemed a good sign; it looked as though there was now no danger of the Japanese breaking through in our direction – by rail at least. We did not have long to wait for some real news.

27 April 1944

I came on duty tonight to find the wards in a very disturbed state. There was nobody to hand over the day report to me and sisters were hurrying about from *basha* to *basha* with dressing trays in their hands. 'What is happening?' I called to Isobel McKenzie, who was preparing a drug at the medication trolley. 'Haven't you heard? Wounded from Kohima,' she answered. 'There's an officer for theatre right away.' I followed her into the ward, where she administered the pre-operative injection to an Indian in the bed at the far end of the room. 'Who is he?' I asked. 'Captain Magid. Both his legs have been blown off and he is being taken to theatre to see if they can save his right arm.' 'Oh God!'

I said. 'How terrible!' 'They had to amputate what remained of his legs two days ago during the fighting. There isn't much hope.'

Captain Magid died on the operating table under the anaesthetic.

Sick and wounded soldiers and airmen from the Fourteenth Army poured into the wards, to be moved on to Dacca and Sirajganj by river as soon as they were fit to travel. I began to question them about their experiences. They told me how, on 4 April, the Japanese 31st Division attacked the British garrison at Kohima, a small town in the jungle terrain of the Naga Hills, not far from the strategically important base at Dimapor. Three days later the enemy cut off the water supply, driving the defenders back to Garrison Hill, where British and American aircraft did their utmost to keep them going with air drops of food, water and ammunition. On 20 April the 6th Brigade of the Second Division broke through the Japanese positions to relieve the garrison, greatly assisted by fighter-bombers from 221 Group, RAF, who had been our neighbours at Asansol.

Some of the seriously wounded, they said, had been flown straight to the military hospitals in India. Often these dogged men, recounting the circumstances of their wounding, would pause, hurriedly light up a rolled cigarette and mumble, 'My mate copped it there,' or 'Sarge had his top half blowed off in that lot.' There was no question of separating surgical and medical cases. The soldier with his jaw shot away could still develop an attack of malaria, for there was a shortage of the specially-proofed mosquito nets, and mepacrine tablets could be forgotten in the heat of battle. Likewise, weary and dispirited men grow careless about the purity of the water they drink or bathe in, inviting parasites of every kind into their intestines. Even at this stage of the war there were twenty cases of tropical illness to one of wounding. On the last day of April a large contingent of Chinese casualties from General Chiang Kai-shek's forces arrived, putting our already overflowing wards under further strain.

A day stands out in my mind, unrecorded in my diary at that time of maximum effort when casualties from a front that stretched seven hundred miles down the middle of Assam produced an unending turnover of patients. There was a British soldier on the surgical ward whose leg wound was infected with staphylococcal bacteria, which were resistent to the sulfa drugs.

Nobody wanted to break the news that his leg must be amputated above the knee in order to save his life. On this particular day all those sisters who could be spared were asked to report to the side ward where the man lay. Major Niblock and Joan Inman were there, dressed as for an operation in gauze masks, sterile gowns and rubber gloves. The major was drawing some yellow liquid into a large syringe. He held it up to the light, saying, 'This is the new drug, which has just arrived. It is called penicillin and we are going to try it out on this patient.'

After carefully cleaning the skin, he injected the drug into a muscle. When we returned three hours later to look at the leg, Major Niblock was saying as he gave the second injection, 'I do believe it looks a little cleaner.' We had heard rumours that an amazing new drug had been discovered at Oxford with the ability to deal with germs that had hitherto been resistent to the sulphonamides – including the dreaded staphylococcus bacterium. Just before going off duty we visited the ward once more and were astonished at the improved state of the wound. There was no longer any doubt – the infection was receding. After five days of three-hourly injections the soldier was able to walk with the help of a stick, finally making a complete recovery.

In the following months I saw penicillin used several times on very ill patients. It was in short supply and therefore as precious as gold but it thoroughly deserved its reputation as the miracle drug of the Second World War.

After a short breathing space to replace casualties, the Fourteenth Army laid siege to Imphal, supported by American Super Fortresses, RAF fighter-bombers and transport aircraft, which also carried out the wounded. By the time the monsoons broke, the Japanese had been driven back, contesting every strip of the jungle until the Imphal area was cleared. 'V' Force from the Arakan had been working their way up towards central Assam, and some of their sick men came to us instead of to the hospitals at Chittagong and Comilla.

One young captain was about as ill as he could be with an as yet undiagnosed fever. Pulse and temperature were very high indeed, making him restless and violent in his movements. I was reminded of the severe lobar pneumonia cases we had nursed at Waterloo Hospital before the sulfa drugs arrived. I sponged his poor wasted body, listening to the low constant mutterings of delirium, alert for any signs, such as rashes or bites, which would give a clue to the cause of his condition.

On lifting his right arm to wash it, I noticed a curious swollen dark-red object, the size of a lentil, attached to the hair under his arm. Captain Grodd recognised the object immediately. It was the tick which caused the type of typhus fever known as scrub typhus.

A diagnosis does not always presage a cure but in this case we were fortunate for, after a week, the young man was able to write a few shaky lines on an airgraph to his mother in Yorkshire. Scrub typhus produces a fearful lassitude and lack of interest in life. I had to put the pen in his hand, coaxing him to scrawl the sentences. How happy I was to be able to add, 'Your son has been ill and is now convalescing. Sister. QAIMNS/R.'

Our third season of hot weather was creeping up on us. Some of us sisters had not been on leave for a year and we were completely drained of energy. Isobel McKenzie was having chest trouble, which led to her leaving the country early the following year; Doris had been in and out of hospital; and I had toothache, which the army dentist's fillings didn't seem to cure. Teddy wrote that a friend of his on the Lopchu Tea Estate at Silchar, not far from Darjeeling, had invited us to stay for a fortnight in his comfortable bungalow within sight of Kanchenjunga. Thus far I had not seen the Himalayas north of Assam and it seemed an opportunity too good to miss. Matron sent me off on my last leave in India with the welcome news that I would be posted to the river steamers when I returned, though I would be expected to work on the wards of the Gauhati hospital between trips.

On the train to Darjeeling we were held up for twenty-four hours in the middle of nowhere by a derailment. As there was nothing else to be had, Teddy and I existed on whisky and water and a tin of corned beef, which we opened with a penknife. The weather was so hot that the corned beef was swimming in its own juice, making it exceedingly difficult to handle, let alone eat. I developed raging toothache, suspected an abscess had formed and applied neat whisky, which had no noticeable effect. My memory of the rest of the journey is vague, but I believe we caught a bus, filled with American servicemen, from Darjeeling to Ghoom, a wet and misty village. Here I bought a waterproof coat but saw nothing of the famous Buddist monastery.

From Ghoom we took a taxi to a milestone ten miles from Kalimpong where we found Mr Creas, our host, waiting with his car. Because of the toothache I was in no state to take in the beauties of the landscape but I dimly remember the stony evidence of landslides on the passing slopes.

Early next morning we went to Darjeeling where the resident English dentist removed my tooth and dealt with the abscess, advising me to go to Pliva's for a brandy and ginger-ale. On the way back to the Lopchu estate I began to recover a little and look around me. Higher and higher we went, splashing over the rivulets that trickled across the track from the rocks above. Great swags of creeper hung in luxuriant folds from the scree. We descended into valleys filled with mist, shivering with cold as icy droplets gathered on the windscreen.

At last we reached the estate and saw across the valley the twin peaks of Kanchenjunga, icily remote against a clear blue sky. Mr Creas told us that we were fortunate to see them as at that time of the year they were often hidden in mist for days. This hospitable estate manager from Scotland, who had worked with tea companies since he was young, was a fine-looking white-haired man in his sixties who had been a widower for ten years. Much to the disgust of the British community, he had lately married a girl from the local tribe, who had worked as a tea picker on the estate. Her name was Jeti and she was nineteen years old. She stayed in the background except at tea-time when she poured tea (produced in their own factory) out of an elegant glass pot, which showed the clear amber liquid to advantage.

Meeting Jeti in the garden one day, I suggested we go for a stroll together. We went down into the valley where the clouds drifted across the horizon like smoke from an invisible train. She spoke English fairly well and we were able to chat together happily. She talked of Mr Creas, to whom she was clearly devoted; when I asked her what would happen if she were left a widow she laughed and said that her husband would leave her well-provided for so that she could marry a man of her choice. There would be many men anxious to marry her, the young beauty assured me, fingering her solid gold ear-rings and tossing back her mane of midnight hair. I was sorry that I never had the opportunity to speak to her in private again during my stay. It must have been a lonely life for her, cut off from her own kind, with the resentfulness of the Indian servants adding to her discomfort.

A rather isolated Eurasian widow of an Englishman who invited Teddy and me to lunch at her neglected tea estate nearby

was so vociferous about the scandal of Jeti and Mr Creas that

The Himalayas, looking westwards from Darjeeling.

we thought she must have wanted to marry him herself. If Jeti had been Mr Creas's live-in mistress or 'old woman', as the female in such liaisons was called, the Eurasian widow would not have turned a hair.

When we next went into Darjeeling, Jeti came too but was not able to enter the sacred precincts of the Planters' Club. She went to the hairdresser to have her magnificent smooth black hair permanently waved to a frizzy mop and her long, almond-shaped nails painted pillar-box red. Afterwards we all had lunch at Pliva's, followed by a trip to the cinema to see Will Hay, Moore Marriot and fat Graham Moffat in *The Ghost of St Michael's*. Jeti loved it.

It took a few days for me to recover from the abscessed tooth but one morning, when the air was like wine, Teddy and I descended the valley to the River Tista, whose tributaries leaped down the mountains in shining cataracts. We gazed upwards and backwards to Kalimpong, its little white houses clinging to a crag facing Kanchenjunga with shadowy Everest beyond. Settled on a stone bridge eating our lunch of Hunter's beef sand-

135

wiches I described to Teddy the dreadful things I had seen and heard in the wards during the past two months. He estimated that there must have been twenty thousand casualties in South East Asia Command already. I was staggered. I thought of a thousand men, ten rows, each with a hundred men in them. 'That many died in Wingate's first campaign,' said Teddy. Then I thought of twenty thousand, line upon line, platoon after platoon, marching into nothingness, their voices fading into infinity. We gazed towards the mountains as though some answer to this nightmare might be found, but they were veiled in mist.

I stood up and spoke aloud the last verse of 'Dover Beach':

> Ah, love, let us be true
> To one another! for the world, which seems
> To lie before us like a land of dreams,
> So various, so beautiful, so new,
> Hath really neither joy, nor love, nor light,
> Nor certitude, nor peace, nor help for pain;
> And we are here as on a darkling plain
> Swept with confused alarms of struggle and flight,
> Where ignorant armies clash by night.

'Matthew Arnold was a lot more optimistic in later life,' said Teddy, hoping to raise my spirits as I trailed after him up the hill.

The following day started with a heavy mist which gradually whitened, turned golden and then gave way before the onslaught of the splendid sun. We set out to walk through Lopcha bazaar into more wooded country. When we told Mr Creas where we were going he insisted on two scouts following us. Before long we found ourselves slipping and sliding down muddy paths. Suddenly I gave a disgusted cry. A short dark worm-like creature was attached to my bare knee, appearing to have come from nowhere. It was standing on its head waving its tail in the air. As I called out, we became aware of more of the creatures slipping down our boots and wriggling on our clothes. The scouts ran up, lighting cigarettes as they came, and quickly applied the burning ends to the leeches. We had to stand on one leg while we removed our boots to get at the vicious little parasites. We changed direction to avoid the pests, circling round through open country where the orange-coloured berries that we had seen growing in the Himalayan foothills at

Bhim Tal twined amongst the bushes. In the cool grasses by the stream where we stopped for lunch I found a single wild strawberry.

Mr Creas called us into his study when we got back to the bungalow. He said it was reported on All-India Radio that four thousand ships and eleven thousand aircraft had crossed the English Channel to attack the Germans. It was D-Day, 6 June 1944.

The time had come for us to return to the plains. Sikkim, I decided, was the most beautiful place I had seen in my life – and the healthiest. When we left Teddy and I had both gained half-a-stone in weight though Teddy was still much too thin. The responsibility of setting up two large hospitals within three years, one of them being the nearest to Kohima and Imphal during the campaigns, had taken its toll of his health. I was not at all happy about him.

Down we came to Darjeeling, where the engines of the miniature mountain railway chuffed up the hillside while a railway employee shovelled sand on the track to help them negotiate the steep incline. From the train we looked down upon the Assam plain – a huge bowl filled to the brim with a thick white mist which appeared to be as solid as cotton wool. Buried under that suffocating heat haze our respective hospitals awaited our return. Teddy came as far as Gauhati with me before setting off by carrier on the 120-mile journey home via Shillong.

Once again the hottest, most trying time of the year was with us. The wards were filled with patients whose illnesses were aggravated by the dusty, dry atmosphere and the high air temperature. Friday 9 June was a day of intense heat. There had been a brief shower of rain, which had had the same effect on the atmosphere as pouring water on a red-hot sheet of metal. I do not think I had ever been so tormented by the climate. My head veil wilted over my sweat-soaked hair; great patches of moisture gathered on my back and round my belt; all my clothes stuck to my body in sodden discomfort; and the skin on my arms and face prickled with the excess sweat that could not evaporate into the moisture-laden air.

A convoy of forty sepoys arrived from the Imphal area during the morning. They were weary, hungry and thirsty; their wounds needed dressing. Most of the Indian orderlies worked like Trojans but one man – a Hindu – stood about, replying to every request I made to him for lime juice for his comrades,

137

'*Hamara kham ne hai.*' ('It is not my job.') I suspected he was using the caste system as an excuse to avoid work on such a hot day. He looked so cool and smartly dressed, standing there with his hands behind his back doing nothing.

One of the dressing bowls slid off the crowded tray, clattering to the floor at his feet. I asked him to pick it up. Predictably he answered, '*Hamara kham ne hai.*' Of its own volition my hand shot up and slapped him hard across the face, knocking him off balance. I stood appalled by what I had done but still angry. He drew himself up to his full height and for a second we regarded each other with astonishment. Then, 'It is not allowed!' he said, his voice trembling, his face pale. 'It is not allowed for you to neglect your comrades!' I replied. He turned away and left the ward.

As soon as I was off duty that evening I went to see the subahdar-major and told him the whole story. 'Sister sahib, do not apologise,' he admonished me. 'British sahibs always wish to apologise. You must say nothing. I myself will move the *badmash* to another ward. But, sister sahib,' he added, leaning forward in a conspiratorial way and lowering his voice an octave, 'do not go alone to sisters' mess for two weeks or three weeks.' He made a movement as though he held a dagger in his hand. 'It is great disgrace for a man to be struck by a woman.'

It was a great disgrace for the orderly and a salutary lesson for me; violence breeds violence. Weeks of fear and embarrassment followed as a result of my loss of control. I was too ashamed to tell my colleagues what I had done – only Doris knew – and I had to wait about for someone to come off duty so that I could cross in safety through the menacing trees to the sisters' mess. I'm sure the orderly suffered too. His pride was hurt, he lost his corporal's stripe and he had to face the wrath of the formidable subahdar-major.

When I reflected on the incident it struck me that if I had been able to speak the language of my orderlies this misunderstanding might not have arisen. I decided to teach myself Urdu and provided myself with a phrase book. Officers and sisters who passed a simple examination in Urdu received a small bonus in their pay allowance. Private lessons were given by *munshis*, teachers who always seemed to be of the same type: small, wiry, white-haired men with spectacles, who inspired respect and often affection in their pupils. They could be seen scurrying through the streets, some wearing hard round velvet caps, others sporting the more political 'Jinnah' forage caps,

The author in 1943.

their large unfurled umbrellas flapping against their frock-coated figures.

21 June 1944

Something rather distressing happened last night. I was being ferried back to the Upper Bungalow by a Sikh ambulance driver. These Sikhs are very smart men with perfectly made *puggarees* on their heads, curled moustaches and beards which are rolled up neatly in a kerchief. They are proud soldiers who tend to keep themselves and their ambulances in tip-top condition. I was all the more surprised, therefore, when the driver of the ambulance, in which I was the only passenger, stopped suddenly, saying that his lights had failed. Certainly we were plunged into darkness in the most isolated part of the two-mile-long journey but not very far from the bungalow. I felt rather frightened and said to the driver, 'Very well, I shall walk.' I got down and started to walk rapidly away from the vehicle, my heart beating fast, my eyes searching the shadows for a would-be assassin lurking in the dark. Into my mind came all the stories of Chandra Bose I had heard. Was I to be kidnapped and held hostage – or quietly murdered and left in a ditch? Whatever happened I intended putting up a fight. I took my surgical scissors out of my top pocket and held them at the ready whilst I walked. After a minute or two I saw the light of the ambulance shining on the road, the vehicle drew level with me and the driver said, '*Tik hai*, Miss sahib, lights work now.' I got back in the ambulance, reaching the Upper Bungalow without further incident, but I was considerably shaken.

I told Doris and Mary King what had happened, asking them if I ought to report the incident to matron. I pointed out that if I didn't say anything the same thing might happen to someone else, with more serious consequences. What if the villains had failed to turn up that night but intended another attempt? I could not be certain that the lights had been switched off for some subversive reason, though it was odd that this had happened when I was alone in the ambulance. Doris wondered if the light failure was the equivalent of the 'running out of petrol' gambit at home, which Mary thought highly unlikely, but her suggestion decided me to tell matron in the morning.

When I put the case before Miss Summerfield she went straight to Colonel Cawthorn and between them they concocted a new rule that sisters should never travel alone in ambulances. I expect the young Sikh got away with a reprimand for not keeping his vehicle in perfect condition. For his sake I hoped my old friend the subahdar-major wouldn't come to hear of the affair.

It was a measure of the trust that normally existed between the Indians and ourselves that, when a sister in one of the Assam hospitals was murdered soon after I came to Gauhati, none of us thought an Indian was responsible. There were men who were attached to the army from many parts of the world whose antecedents were unknown, any one of whom could have been the perpetrator of the deed. It could equally well have been a perfectly respectable member of the hospital community who suffered a sudden aberration under stress. The sister was crossing over from the hospital to the mess after evening duty when she was set upon, dragged to a hut and killed. Another sister found her handbag, with the letter she had written to her mother that evening spilling out of it at the side of the path, and gave the alarm. As far as I know, the man who committed the crime was never found. The reason I heard about the affair was that two sisters from the hospital where the murder took place were posted to us. They had been asked not to discuss it, but I overheard them talking.

At the beginning of July, an unhealthy month at the best of times, we found ourselves in the middle of a cholera epidemic. The rain washed infected material into rivers and wells so that those people who did not boil their water were at risk. Summoned to the cholera ward in order to familiarise ourselves with the appearance of the bacteria, we watched with a morbid fascination the small curved comma-bacillus wriggling about under the microscope. Who would have thought such an insignificant speck could cause such havoc. My mind went back to my training when, on a bitterly cold day with windows grey with frost, we probationers heard the story of Robert Koch, who first identified the true Asiatic cholera germ, *Vibrio Cholerae*, in 1883. Before that date cholera had been frequently confused with dysenteries, which presented similar symptoms. But cholera is far more dangerous to the community it invades than any outbreak of dysentery.

Mary King and I entered the large isolation *basha* where the beds were dotted about the room to make access to the bedside easy for the sweepers. Each patient lay on a wooden bed-frame, whose coir-rope supports held the emaciated bodies as in a hammock. Under each bed stood a large bowl to catch the continual gushes of 'rice-water' motions, which produced dehydration in the victim. The mosquito nets reached to the floor to prevent the entry of flies.

Colonel Ransome was putting a saline intravenous drip on

the patient nearest the door. The veins of the arm had collapsed and he hunted round the body to find a means of access to pour new life into a fluid-drained shell. That smart and vital doctor looked tired and pale, with a day's growth of beard detracting from the jauntiness of his handlebar moustache. From all around came the groans of patients suffering from painful cramps in the muscles of the arms, legs and abdomen, mingled with the sounds of vomiting and intense purging. Patiently the little band of carefully instructed sweepers went about their horrid task of emptying and renewing bowls. So must the wards of Scutari have looked to the Crimean nurses.

Only a small number of sisters, protected by gowns and gloves, were allowed to carry out monitoring procedures such as checking pulses and taking temperatures. At the acute stage of the illness there was very little more that could be done, but the convalescent period offered wide scope for nursing skills.

All ten of the Indian patients that Mary and I saw that day survived; some had a natural partial resistance to the cholera germ, others were certainly saved by the saline drips. The normally silent Mary King came to life over this traumatic episode, revealing depths of feeling that I for one had not known existed in her. Behind that calm face with its perfect features dwelt a personality that slept like a '*princesse lointaine*', waiting to be awakened by the right circumstances or person into a joyous vitality. I hoped that I would be around to see it happen.

With the end of the cholera outbreak in August, social life continued as before. The various army and air force units in the area put on parties at the weekends where we played games, such as guessing from pictures cut out of old magazines what advertisements they represented. The men always let the women win, awarding a small prize – usually a powder compact or ear-rings – to the one with the highest score. Returning one night from such a party in an open jeep, our headlamps picked out the dim mottled shape of a large animal crossing the road ahead of us. It was a leopard out foraging for small deer or wild pig. We thought it advisable to avoid pulling up to inspect it further.

At the wheel on these occasions was a Greek officer called Angelo, who was a splendid driver and very abstemious. Angelo was endowed with other talents: he was the only man I met in India who could dance the tango properly.

Teddy wrote to say that he had been before a medical board and had been given eight months' sick leave in Canada. He enclosed a charming letter from his mother to me, saying how pleased she was her son had found happiness. If I was still adamant about not marrying until the war was over, would I at least meet him in Calcutta so that we could buy an engagement ring? In April 1945 he would be back there for our wedding. If the war finished earlier we would make other plans.

I reminded matron that she had promised me a permanent posting to the river steamer unit, persuading the senior steamer sister, Dorothy Baker, to put in a good word for me. Miss Summerfield agreed to let me go. The sisters at the Upper Bungalow were gradually being dispersed, moving forward with the changed tide of battle. Marty Adair and Monica Lamb were sent on leave before being posted to the 15th Casualty Clearing Station in the Arakan. Mary King took her mysterious self to an unknown destination and only Doris remained to greet me whenever the steamer docked at Gauhati.

5 · On the River

The uninspiring wood and bamboo headquarters of the Indian Hospital River Steamers stood on the quayside of the Brahmaputra River, a short distance from the Gauhati hospital. Major Mayne, the CO of this unit, a tall stooping RAMC officer not far from retirement, sat in his dark office organising the transportation of convoys by ambulance and truck from the 52nd Combined Military Hospital to the decks of the river steamers. There was little to relieve the monotony of the sun-bleached *ghat* (jetty). The only shade came from a thickset tree that was hung about with great coarse moss-green jack-fruits, whose rank odour was so offensive to British noses.

Major Mayne was assisted in his duties by two young RAMC sergeants, Owen and curly-haired Pilgrim, who personally supervised the transfer of the weaker patients from ambulances to steamer bunks by stretcher, proffering a cigarette here, a word of encouragement there as they steered the sepoy stretcher-bearers over the narrow gangplanks.

The steamer unit consisted of eight paddle-steamers with large Red Cross markings on their wooden canopies to discourage Japanese bombers. The ships' engines were most reliable, although they had been assembled on Clydeside and brought out to the Bay of Bengal in the nineteenth century. Each ship was self-contained with a medical officer (British or Indian) in command; two QA sisters, if they could be spared, otherwise one sister and one Anglo-Indian nurse; one British orderly and several Indian orderlies; lastly, a crew that seemed to consist of representatives of every nation east of Suez. The ships' masters were always Muslims from Chittagong, strict disciplinarians who saw to it that their mainly Muslim crew kept all the feasts and fasts of their religion with due ceremony. Many of the masters were related to each other. It was said that the master of our steamer used to beat his youngest brother, who was the master of another ship, whenever the two steamers

145

put in at the same port. The youngest brother was around fifty years of age. With their long white flowing beards they looked like Old Testament prophets, but their black embroidered waistcoats and red fez hats added a swashbuckling element to their appearance.

Accommodation for patients and staff varied from one ship to another. Most had bunks for over a hundred soldiers, while the staff, whose home the steamer was for up to a week at a time, had a dining saloon with a small foredeck, a cabin each, a small kitchen and a bathroom with a real bath. The British orderly had a minute cabin on the main deck. Some steamers were quite spartan, with bare decks where the stretchers were laid in rows and inferior staff accommodation. The Hindus and Muslims had their own cookhouses on the lower deck, both so tiny that it was impossible to imagine how meals for sixty or more patients could be produced. An Indian havildar was in charge of the dry stores and Red Cross supplies, issuing them in conjunction with the medical officer. No words can say how grateful we were to the Red Cross organisation for all they supplied: face-flannels and toothbrushes; soap and razors; socks and pyjamas; and even exotic things like port and brandy. Now and again we found a note tucked into the toe of a sock, giving the name of the knitter and of a town in the United Kingdom. This pleased everybody beyond belief. Not only did it make us feel in touch with our suppliers of small luxuries; it also assured us that life was going on in a normal way at home.

In the prow of the ship stood a member of the crew with a graduated pole, whose business it was to measure the depth of the water, particularly when the channel was narrow. He shouted, or rather intoned, the measurements in a rhythmic manner, rather like a religious chant, and the mournful dirge accompanied our progress by day and night. The master was frequently to be seen aloft surveying his kingdom, his long white beard streaming in the wind, his hawk's eye alert for signs of sandbanks ahead. His chief responsibility must have been the avoidance of such obstacles, which were constantly shifting in monsoon weather when the river was in spate. Overnight it could change from a reasonably well-behaved, normal-sized stream to a raging torrent a mile wide. Sometimes, despite the master's endeavours, we drifted on to a sandbank but he always managed to free us after a great deal of shouting, clanging of bells and reversing. He showed us a paddy-field where, a few years previously, one of the steamers was left high and dry in the night, the river having whimsically altered its course.

Because of the influx of patients from the battle area during the hot weather and monsoon season of 1944, steamer sisters had to report to the Gauhati hospital as soon as they returned from a voyage; one could work all day on the wards and then be required to go on board the steamer at 6pm, remaining on duty for three days. This was probably one reason why regular steamer postings were not particularly sought after, the other being that some sisters were unwilling to be cut off from semi-civilisation and the company of their own kind for up to six days at a time and preferred the ward routine to a more unpredictable way of life.

The end of June found me on the *Mikir*, one of the least comfortable of the steamers, though two tiers of bunks had been introduced for the patients. Most of the sick and wounded from Kohima and Imphal had passed down the river to India. Chindits who had come out of Burma via Dinjan airfield and Panitola hospital in the north now began to arrive in their hundreds. On this trip we carried ten gunners from Assam and sixty Chindits with two very ill officers. They filled every available space, many of them lying wearily on their straw mattresses gazing at the passing scenery, only too glad to be in an area where they were safe from sudden death. Most of them looked like skeletons as a result of dysentery, malaria and general privation. It was pathetic to see these bundles of skin and bone trying to eat the good meals provided – chicken broth and canned pears being the favourites. They would ask for a generous helping, start to eat avidly, then put the plate down with regret, their stomachs not able to cope with anything stronger than milk dishes and eggs.

In the evening I listened to the men from the Lancashire Fusiliers and the Leicester Regiment who came up to the serving hatch for the rum ration and a good 'dekko' at a genuine British female. I noticed that the tough little city dwellers had come off better than the larger country boys in the type of warfare they were exposed to. The former, no doubt, had learned about survival in the hard school of the asphalt jungle and were quicker in their response to danger. There was a powerful feeling of comradeship amongst these soldiers who had gone through so much together.

Sometimes when a man could not sleep he would wander along the deck seeking not a pill for insomnia but a comforting mug of char. He would tell me as he savoured the reassuring beverage how the brew-ups and fags were the only things that made life bearable in the jungle. Then he might speak of his training days, recalling how the 'kite-hawks' swooped down to snatch chicken legs from the soldiers' tin plates or how the monsoon rains started with a wind that caused half the tents to collapse, leaving the trainees exposed to the elements.

One of the Chindits, whose closest friend had been killed before his eyes by a burst of fire from an enemy ambush, told me of the doubtful blessings of sleep in a foxhole dug out of a hillside, wrapped in the same wet waterproof cape that he had marched in all day. His feet became so swollen that he dare not remove his wet boots in case he could not get them back on in the morning. These men lived on American 'K' rations until they hated the sight of them – though they were vastly superior to the British packs – and longed for the air drops that supplied them with such luxuries as canned fruit, rum and cigarettes.

Having transferred our Chindits and the other small group of Fourteenth Army men to the ambulance train at Sirajganj after the thirty-six hour voyage, the *Mikir* started off on its return journey to Gauhati. The absence of patients gave me the opportunity to begin learning Urdu with the help of Nurse Mary de Souza, my assistant on the steamer, a plump and swar-thy lady from Goa with fine dark eyes inherited from her south-Indian father. As I was the only Westerner on board I decided to adapt myself to the Indian way of life, learning from Mary how to wear a sari and listening to Indian music; but my attempt at Indian dancing so amused my instructor that the tears poured down her face. Captain Pillai of the Indian Army Medi-cal Services, a short, very dark-skinned man from Madras, ordered Indian food for me and I came to appreciate hotter south-Indian curries and exotic condiments, only the sweet-meats proving too sugary for my taste. I found myself adopting a slower, more relaxed attitude to life, removed as I was from my usual social contacts and hospital ward crises.

The evenings on the foredeck were delightful. They were spent listening to stories of Hindu gods and goddesses, though Mary, who was a Goanese Christian, assured me that they were symbolic tales, parables of instruction like those in our New Testament. Later we would fall silent, gazing riverwards at the sampans silhouetted against a primrose sky. The village huts, like nests at the foot of mop-headed palms, the thick jungle coming down to the water's edge, the rocky islands in midstream were all transformed by the rays of the setting sun which, during the monsoon season, had that rare quality of changing and heightening the colours of land and water.

It was strange to return to the Gauhati hospital after the three-day trip, laying aside my Indian persona with my borrowed sari until the next voyage. Invitations were waiting for me when I looked for my mail in the sisters' mess, one of them from the American headquarters where a film show was to be held that evening. Several doctors and sisters went along, sitting in an exceedingly crowded hall in order to watch the antics of a youthful Micky Rooney in *Girl Crazy*, followed by a highly patriotic war film in which Gregory Peck, I think it was, won the campaign in the South Pacific single-handed. Afterwards some of the enlisted men came over to talk to us. On our enquiring what GI stood for they replied, 'General Issue', which we found unconvincing, deciding that they were pulling our legs. One of their number, Charlie Bock, who looked like a shorter, darker and less menacing Humphrey Bogart, asked me if the British soldiers on the steamers would like some Lucky Strike cigarettes. Knowing how welcome such an offer would be, I accepted on their behalf. Charlie was waiting on the *ghat* when I went down to the river to join my steamer two days later, his arms extended round several giant cans of Californian orange juice for the staff and four enormous cartons of cigarettes for the patients. Dr Pillai, Mary and I appreciated the fruit juice, which made a change from the eternal *nimbu pani*. We set aside some tins for ill patients and distributed the cigarettes to the soldiers, who rejoiced over such an unexpected windfall.

From then on Charlie adopted us, appearing with fresh supplies every time the *Mikir* docked. On one occasion Captain Pillai invited him to share our evening meal of goat stew. He accepted with alacrity but when he started to eat I saw that he had a plaster cast on his right wrist. He explained that he had broken it a few days earlier doing something to an aeroplane and I had to cut up his meat for him, which made him blush like a schoolgirl. Fascinated as I was by other cultures, I liked to hear Charlie's descriptions of the American way of life at home and in India. I think he came from Ohio but I am not at all sure. What I am sure about is that he had an innocent and generous nature and was as different from the stereotyped image of the brash American GI as could possibly be imagined.

At this stage of the war, with so many doctors both British and Indian posted to the battle areas, the river steamer unit had to make use of licentiates – partly-trained Indians with a knowledge of surgical techniques, drug treatments and first aid. They were simple village doctors, perfectly suited to the supervision of patients on the move from one hospital to another. One of these men arrived at our unit. Major Mayne explained that he was sending me out on the *Mallard* with Mary de Souza and was relying on me to make the new licentiate doctor *au fait* with shipboard routines.

Early in August we sailed from Gauhati with a hundred British and Indian patients from Burma. It was a hot night with sudden downpours of rain and the orderlies had to lower the canvas awnings to keep the deck patients dry. I was called up in the early hours by the Indian night orderly. He led me to a British soldier on a top bunk who was fast sinking into a coma caused by cerebral malaria. Having sent the orderly to waken the doctor, I prepared the routine standard dose of intravenous quinine in a syringe. I offered it to the doctor as he approached, pale and dishevelled, struggling with his recalcitrant dressing gown. He mumbled something about the quinine not being needed just yet, leaving me in a quandary. If the soldier didn't have the injection pretty soon he would die. We were still a day's journey from Sirajganj so there was no chance of his getting the quinine from someone else until it was too late.

As we stood there looking at the patient by the dim rays of a kerosene lamp, it suddenly dawned on me that the licentiate doctor had never given an intravenous injection before. This was the moment I had dreaded. I said, 'If you like, I will do it myself,' and I meant it; but I was not sorry when he took the syringe from me, injecting the quinine into a vein in the patient's arm in a perfectly satisfactory manner. Shortly afterwards the soldier regained consciousness to the relief of all concerned.

A barrier was broken down between the licentiate doctor and myself on that occasion. I cannot remember the man's name as I had only one voyage with him but he confessed to being partly European – Portuguese, I believe – so he and Mary had something in common. The return journey to Gauhati was to provide him with another emergency to cope with.

The lower deck held livestock for consumption during the voyage; thus, apart from the throbbing of the engines, the chanting of prayers and the intoning of the man with the graduated pole, there was a constant clucking of hens, quacking of ducks and bleating of goats. The crew had a pet goat as big as a Shetland pony, which we called Billy-Goat Gruff. He was an evil-looking creature with blank yellow eyes whose days were spent in wandering round the lower deck nibbling at our vegetable rations. When I went down to inspect the food in the galley I waited until he was looking the other way before I crossed the deck as I thought he might take it into his wicked old head to butt me in the back.

On the second day of the return voyage, while the cook squatted on the edge of the lower deck eating his curry and rice, the goat came up behind him, gave a few playful trots and butted him into the Brahmaputra. Pandemonium broke loose. The master, heaving his large bulk out of the bunk where he was having a siesta, took control of the situation at once by reversing the engines and backing to the place where the unfortunate cook waved his arms and cried that he was drowned. He was in such a poor condition when pulled from the river that the licentiate doctor poured some Red Cross brandy gently down his throat. With all the excitement, no one remembered to say that Abdul Aziz was a Muslim, alcohol being anathema to him.

The next day Abdul appeared to be none the worse for his immersion in the Brahmaputra for he was working in the galley as usual; but in the evening he began to pray very loudly so that his accusing cries rose up like incense until they reached the ears of the licentiate on the top deck. It was difficult to know who felt the more guilt – Abdul Aziz or the doctor.

As for the villain of the piece, the egregious Billy-Goat Gruff, he developed pneumonia, responding not at all to the sulfa drugs he was given. I watched him struggling for breath as he lay on his side on an old blanket on the deck, his wicked eyes devoid of anything that could be described as emotion or awareness in the human sense, and found it in my heart to be sorry for him. I decided that the reason the crew hadn't slaughtered the goat was that they were afraid of him, not because they regarded him as a pet. Had pneumonia not supervened he might have continued to consume the vegetable rations with impunity for many years. The crew clustered round the deathbed of Billy-Goat Gruff watching him breathe his last. Even the old Muslim cook came to pay his respects. I left them together and crept upstairs to see what was happening to my other patients.

Next day we were served goat stew for dinner. As I lifted my fork to my mouth I thought of something. I hurried downstairs to interview the cook, but after a few tentative enquiries discovered that the goat's carcass had not gone ignominiously into the cooking pot. The cook looked slightly affronted at my insinuations, assuring me that the deceased animal had been tied up in his own blanket and consigned to the all-embracing Brahmaputra River.

After that river trip Mary and the licentiate were posted elsewhere and I never saw them again. The *Mallard* was taken over by Captain Hennessy RAMC, a strapping Irishman with a wife and two children who lived in Middlesborough, Yorkshire. He was in his early thirties, the same age as Gwen Hallett, who joined the *Mallard* at that time as senior sister, regretfully leaving all her friends at the 17th British General Hospital, Dacca.

Until September 1944 Sirajganj had been our Mecca, so to speak; but now we were to range further afield about every second trip, to Dacca, the capital of East Bengal, a three-day journey from Gauhati. Fortified by the customary offerings of orange juice, books and cigarettes from Charlie Bock, we set out with the highest number of patients we had ever carried. There were 172 of them, half being what the Indians called *pagals*, mentally-ill sepoys for whom the separation from familiar surroundings and people, or the experience of warfare, had proved too taxing. Mostly they were sad quiet men suffering from depression. I had read beginner's textbooks on the theories of Freud, Jung and Adler but they did not seem to relate to my childlike silent patients, who almost appeared to be hibernating. Those who were a danger to themselves or others occupied the large wire-mesh cage at one end of the deck which was otherwise used for prisoners of war.

7 September 1944

Today there is a rowdy couple in the cage putting on a drama that is watched with interest even by the depressed patients. One of them is a huge Pathan from north India with a tremendous voice, who is keeping everyone from sleeping whilst he taunts the diminutive Hindu half his size who shares his cage. The poor little man appears to be in abject terror as he crouches in the corner, pleading in a treble voice. We offered to let the little man out but he

Porters at work, Dhubri ghat, 1945.

refused to budge. There is evidently some sort of satisfying relationship between the two – the one bullying, the other bullied – which we find hard to understand. The 'sadism' of one and the 'masochism' of the other produce a relationship of some sort, but an exceedingly unbalanced one.

When the Hindu was given food, the Pathan took it from him, chasing him noisily round the cage. In the end we persuaded the Pathan to swallow a dose of bromide, after which he quietened down and suddenly fell asleep, making it possible for the Hindu to eat a square meal. He looked

The author and Captain James Hennessy RAMC near the statue of Queen Victoria, Dhubri, 1944.

rather lost and lonely with no one to bully him, evidently missing the security of being part of the big strong Pathan.

We felt sure that most of these disturbed sepoys would recover once they were back in a familiar environment with the village sights and sounds around them. Only those men with a strong feeling of selfhood appeared to face completely new circumstances without suffering some degree of disorientation. When possible, soldiers with the same background, whether ethnic or religious, were kept together to support each other as they faced the hardships and dangers of jungle warfare.

After sailing for a day and a night, we reached Dhubri, our first port of call from Gauhati – though that would be an inflated description of the small bazaar with its river frontage of parched grass. A rough path led up to a railed garden whose centrepiece was an imposing metal statue of Queen Victoria in her heyday bearing a crown and sceptre. Every year on the feast of Holi, Havildar Husain told us, the local Indians painted

Hospital river steamer staff beside an ambulance train, Sirajganj, 1944.
Gwen Hallett, Jim Hennessy, the author.

the statue red, though whether this was an insult or a compliment to Her Imperial Majesty we could not make out.

Only a handful of patients left the ship but we remained at anchor for an hour or two while the coal for the ship's furnace was taken aboard. Two planks were placed from the river bank to a hatch on deck to allow a long line of coolies, each carrying a shallow basket of coal on his rag-protected head, to run along the springy boards and tip his burden into the hold. The coolies were very thin and wiry. Their bulky loincloths absorbed the rivulets of sweat that poured down their spines. They formed a dark frieze against the sky as they ran on and on like a piece of well-oiled machinery.

We three staff went on shore to stretch our legs. An aged *chokidar* came to meet us bearing a large rusty key which he waved before him to draw us towards the small European club house set back behind the garden. Inside he introduced us to a small bar (closed), an old gramophone (open) and a well-polished dance floor not more than a few yards square. We

155

gingerly put on a record from the stack provided, surprised to find that it was the up-to-date 'Anniversary Waltz' instead of a Viennese waltz from Queen Victoria's time. The three of us danced round the floor with imaginary partners before locking up the club house and handing over the ancient key to the waiting *chokidar*. There were obviously a few British residents around, probably connected with the Inland Water Transport, which was run by Europeans.

The whole place had an air of having been left behind by the last century. The garden was untended but we found a few English flowers running to seed, perhaps introduced and nurtured by some long-dead memsahib. Nostalgically we gathered a few cornflowers, marigolds and monkshood from a bygone age to adorn our saloon, then closed the creaking gate leaving the garden to its dreams.

Further along the *ghat* were the largest ant hills we had ever seen: black earth-cones of fervid activity, towering taller than a man. I shuddered at the thought of someone pushing over the heap of soil to release millions of termites which would surge towards us from the chambers and underground passages of the ant city. When we reached the bazaar we found that it consisted of one short street of booths, whose chief attractions were a photographer and a busy barber's shop – busy because Indian males never seemed to shave themselves but employed a barber, who sat outside plying his trade. Captain Hennessy, Gwen Hallett and I went in to have our picture taken.

After an uneventful few hours' sailing we reached Sirajganj *ghat*, a God-forsaken spot without amenities of any sort. Along the shore the wind stirred up dust-devils, spirals of dry particles that swirled into the air to the height of several feet before suddenly collapsing. Captain Anrep RAMC came out of his lonely *basha* to greet us, a quiet interesting-looking man in his late twenties, dressed in the routine daytime khaki shirt, shorts and knee socks. His particular job as a doctor was to see that the patients were safely transferred from the *Mallard* to the ambulance train that stood on the *ghat* ready to carry them on to the 67th Indian General Hospital about eight miles away.

Captain Anrep showed us round his train and took us to his *basha* for a drink before joining us for a mixed-grill supper on board. With a British sergeant and a group of Sikh ambulance drivers he made the best of a somewhat dreary existence in those desolate marshes, looking forward to the arrival of the steamers as the highlight of his week. He had trained at University College Hospital, London, and had spent his time in India being moved from one temporary job to another, feeling that he would have been more use at home in wartime London. From his conversation we thought that he might have left behind in England a rather special girlfriend. Reluctantly Captain Anrep returned to his sad cargo of *pagals*, already settled in the ambulance train on their way to safety and – we hoped – sanity.

We were hardly out of sight of Sirajganj when our ship developed engine trouble. We anchored close to the shore, where the village children quickly formed a team, plunging into the water the better to make their high-pitched demands for bread and annas audible to everyone on the steamer. The crew, having been made to clean the ship from stem to stern, found many tasty titbits to throw to the laughing children. In the midst of this frolicking social occasion two snake-charmers arrived, settled themselves down on the bank and started their monotonous pipe music.

We had a pet mongoose on board – sworn enemy of snakes – of whom we were all very fond, even though he had an annoying habit of rolling our breakfast eggs out of our store cupboard in order to eat them himself. This mongoose, who looked rather like an English ferret, roamed the decks at will. Intrigued by the pipe music, he sneaked over the gangplank and seized one of the gyrating cobras by the neck. A tremendous battle took place amidst howls of encouragement from the bystanders. The two snake-charmers wailed helplessly, rocking to and fro on their haunches and making not the slightest attempt to part the combatants. The little mongoose held on until the snake collapsed in a limp coil.

Immediately the snake owners came out of their torpor, stretching their arms towards us as we watched from the top deck and demanding damages to the extent of ten rupees – a small fortune to them, but not a prohibitive sum to us. The money was handed over, to be tucked carefully inside their turbans. As they hurried away with their baskets swinging on a bamboo pole carried between them, I distinctly saw the 'dead' cobra moving around its wicker cage. It struck us that the failure of the ship's engines had coincided with the advent of the snake-charmers. We began to suspect that the episode had been planned and that some members of the crew would have benefited financially from the generosity of the medical officer and sisters. We even wondered about the attack by Rikki-tikki-tavi, the mongoose; perhaps he had been inveigled off the ship by interested persons to help put on a good show.

A day's voyage beyond Sirajganj, on the left-hand bank of the Burhi Ganga, sprawled Dacca, the university city of East Bengal. I came to prefer this stretch of water to all others I sailed on. The stream was narrow and winding, carrying us between low green banks where the ship almost touched the sides during our slow progression. From the passing villages it must have appeared as though we were sailing through the fields, so tenuous was the channel. I loved to spend my afternoon off-duty time lying on a camp bed on the foredeck outside our saloon, watching the lush verdant banks change in character with each bend in the river. Sometimes the trees, bright with tropical purples and scarlets, came down to the water's edge; sometimes they receded to reveal tiny village settlements with children playing and women washing clothes on the stone steps built into the bank. I used to reflect as I lay there that a thousand years could come and go yet those scenes would remain the same, the women in their white or earth-coloured saris balancing water-pots on their heads, the children in their short shifts, bare-legged and bare-bottomed, with the odd pai dog rooting about in the rubbish. It always seemed to be perfect weather, softly warm with a faint breeze, and it was easy to drift into sleep.

On very hot nights, which occurred even in September, Gwen Hallett and I slept on the deck with mosquito nets as a protection against the insects that rained on to the ship, attracted by the searchlight on the prow. Sometimes I tried to count the different varieties but I soon gave up in despair; one armoured creature was at large as a frog – well, not a fully-grown frog – and if I had not so much disliked killing them with our baseball bat I would have started a collection with him.

My face was still disfigured by a scar from what the Indians called a 'spider's lick'. This unpleasant centipede-like creature sprayed a fluid on exposed skin surfaces, causing an extraordinarily painful blister which, after a few days, looked like a neglected cold-sore. Ever afterwards in monsoon weather I examined the inside of my mosquito net before retiring. Despite the constant pattering of the insects on the deck, Gwen and I did manage to get some sleep, though there was always the possibility of being awakened in the small hours by a sudden squall. These tremendous rainstorms blew in from the Bay of Bengal without warning. The wind lifted the mosquito nets,

The author shopping in Dacca bazaar, October 1944.

carrying them away over the river and tearing at the sheets. We wrapped them tightly round us as, buffeted by the gale, we staggered to our cabins drenched to the skin.

On the third day out from Gauhati our steamer anchored amongst all the other ships and launches along the Dacca waterfront. The rest of our patients were unloaded within an hour on to train, truck or ambulance for the 17th British General Hospital a mile or so away. They were mostly walking cases

159

and had enjoyed the trip tremendously. Gwen and I went by tricycle rickshaw to the bazaar, where they sold spangles, bangles, exotic jewellery and handsome cocktail shakers of Benares brass, one of which I bought. Then we went on to the swimming pool. Gwen, who was a splendid swimmer, told me that she was brought up in Lyme Regis where there were excellent opportunities for water sports. I felt rather relieved that she had not been on the *Mallard* when the cook was butted into the river; I could imagine her diving in fully-clothed and swimming back to rescue him. Gwen was no beauty but she had a fine strong body and a cheerful unselfish nature; she was the one who lifted the spirits of the troops with a joke and kept everyone in a good humour in bad weather, devising games to play and ransacking the Red Cross stores for 'extras' for the ill patients.

In the evening a friendly jute manager, Mr McKentish, whose large stone-built house backed on to the quay, invited us to dine with him. He was a rubicund jovial man in his sixties who had lived in India since he left Scotland in his youth to be apprenticed to the jute trade. If he had a wife she must have been away in the hills. He looked forward to meeting anyone from the United Kingdom brought in by the steamers, entertaining them to opulent meals organised by his excellent *khitmagar* (butler). After dinner he took us in his own launch to the club at Narayangunj further downstream, where bagpipes were being played to a mainly Scottish audience. (Every club in India seemed to have a high proportion of Scots members.) There was plenty of whisky flowing and Captain Hennessy was able to do full justice to it, keeping up with Mr McKentish drink for drink. As we made our rather meandering way back along the river, I commented on the water hyacinths that spread like a green meadow, thick with blue-mauve flowers, which covered the surface around the Dacca quay. Mr McKentish said that it might be a sight to inspire a poet but it cost the shipping companies a great deal of money as the long tough stems could foul a propeller. All his jute products were carried by water, many of them being used to help the war effort, such as hessian cloth for packing weapons, gunny bags and cording ropes. It was midnight when we reached the quay, where we thanked Mr McKentish for his hospitality, promising to give a party for him on the *Mallard* on our next visit.

Before we left, the Deputy Director of Medical Services called on us to check that no unauthorised passengers were lurking on board. We were only allowed to carry noncombatants as we were a hospital ship, bound by the rules of the Geneva Convention. Anyone who tried to cadge a lift by crossing the gangplank with a false pass or a feigned limp was given short shrift by Captain Hennessy. The steamer felt strangely quiet and empty after the turmoil of Dacca. Back we sailed through the narrow channel, making the most of the fresh morning air before the sun drained the atmosphere with its vampire rays. When we reached Sirajganj, Ted Calder, a young man working with the Inland Water Transport, offered to take us a few miles across the countryside in his motor car – a rare vehicle in those parts – setting us free to walk back to the *ghat* at our leisure.

The landscape was as flat and featureless as we had been led to believe. As we stood in a stubble field gazing around us, an aged peasant appeared from nowhere, hurrying forward with a battered camp stool for the sahib to sit on. Captain Hennessy demurred but Gwen and I insisted that he should sit down to please the old man, who stood at the salute. I thought the Indian must have served with the army fifty years earlier under the Queen Empress and was showing his respect for a pukka officer sahib – or perhaps he merely hoped for baksheesh. I was about to ask Gwen's opinion when suddenly, from over the fields, came a loud hoot from the *Mallard*, which was the signal for departure. Wondering what had happened on board to make our return imperative, we demonstrated in mime to the old man that we needed some form of transport, whereupon he set off across the field as fast as his spindly legs would let him, beckoning us on with encouraging chatter until we reached a small hamlet. There we negotiated for their only two bicycles, vintage 1920, promising to send them back before nightfall (word of a sahib, accepted unreservedly). After a rough ride, punctuated by outbursts of exasperation and hilarity, we made it to the jetty.

Major Mayne, who had boarded the steamer in our absence, had news for us, relayed to him by Ted Calder, who picked up his information at the river transport headquarters. The Fourteenth Army had crossed the Chindwin river in Burma, driving the Japanese before it and was approaching the Irrawaddy river. Major Mayne was anxious to get back to Gauhati in order to have the report confirmed. After paying two men to return the bone-shaker bicycles to their owners, we cast off for home, our last sight of Sirajganj revealing a couple of meandering figures perched precariously on the ancient machines disappearing into the sunset.

19 September 1944

We are approaching Gauhati once more. This is the most
beautiful of nights. Ahead of us curves the moon, a silver
thread of light flanked by a single star which proclaims to
the Muslim world the advent of Id al Fitr and the end of
their long fast. The sky is a lucent indigo, drawing its light
from the increasing stars rather than from the fragile moon.
Like the new fire of Easter in the Western world, this
festival speaks of the possibility of a fresh start in life. It is
a time for hope and trust in the future.

In the morning when we docked opposite Major Mayne's headquarters the master with members of his crew came to the
saloon to wish us happiness, presenting us with flowers and
sweetmeats. It was impossible not to be moved by such spontan-
eous joy and we parted with salaams on either side. Later we
contributed to a feast for the crew, who always worked so hard
in the background making it possible for thousands of patients
to reach a place of care and safety.

We remained in Gauhati for a week while the *Mallard* had
her boilers cleaned at Gaolundo, near Dhubri. There was a
parcel from my Canadian aunt waiting for me, containing a
cotton frock, white with green and orange stripes, tight-
bodiced and full-skirted – quite different from the utility-type
mufti clothes we were wearing. Also there were three pairs of
the new nylon stockings.

One of a batch of letters from Teddy explained that he planned to meet the steamer at Dacca on our next trip as he would
be working at the Comilla military hospital until he left for
Canada. Then there were the usual invitations to warrant officers' and British other ranks' dances, this time to celebrate the
arrival of the first English VADs – just two of them to begin
with but with the promise of more to follow. Lastly there was
a letter from Marty Adair at the 15th Casualty Clearing Station,
Arakan Yoma, addressed to Doris Oliver and me, telling us
of the high incidence of scrub typhus cases in the area and
expressing the hope that she would meet us in Calcutta one
day.

After a week on duty with the *pagals* on Block Six Gwen
and I were called back to the *Mallard* for our last trip of the

A sampan on the River Brahmaputra.

monsoon season. This time there was a large contingent of
Indian other ranks bound for Sirajganj and Dacca, according
to whether their illnesses were of the mind or the body. We
left at 6pm after a day's work. When we had fed the patients,
issued the orderlies with the rum ration for the non-Muslim
patients and settled everybody down, Gwen and I sat on the
foredeck discussing which of us should be on call for the first
night on board. Only the muted pulse of the ship's engines and
the soft shuffle of the prow's progress through the channel disturbed the quiet air. I took out my diary to record my impressions of a familiar and much-loved landmark :

> We are approaching the little island that is sacred to the
> Hindus. It stands in the middle of the river, parting the
> flood of water on either side, and its beauty is so mysterious

163

that I long to land on it alone. Steep and craggy at its base with white rocks rising sheer out of the flood, it softens into green feathery trees and cliff-hanging shrubs higher up. It looks like an Arthur Rackham illustration of a magic fortress and I am convinced that there must be a ruined castle or temple hidden away on top. It always seems to be late evening or sunset as our ship makes a wide detour to sail round the island at the start of a voyage. This evening a soft breeze springs up to remind us how fortunate we are to have escaped a suffocatingly hot night on shore. The moon, larger and more golden than the harvest moons of England, peers above the island as it gathers the evening mists around it and slips into the night.

About three hundred miles and two days later we reached Siraj-ganj just in time for Captain Anrep to get the patients to hospital on the last train of the day. We changed out of our sweat-soaked khaki and sat on the deck nursing cool, gin-flavoured *nimbu panis*, except for Gwen who never drank alcohol of any kind. Igor Anrep was somewhat preoccupied. I noticed him glancing towards the shore and regarding each of us speculatively with his somewhat enigmatic dark brown eyes. After a pause in the conversation he swivelled his chair round and pointed out a little Indian boy who was standing on the *ghat* amongst the dust-devils that swirled like dancing dervishes.

'That is Noor Din,' he said abruptly. 'He's twelve though he doesn't look it. He needs a job. How would you like him for a batman?' He addressed Jim Hennessy but included all of us in his appeal. Gwen and I exchanged looks. We had seen the hungry children by the river, emaciated, with abdomens swollen from enlarged malarial livers; they waited stolidly for handouts from the steamers – bread, fruit, rice, anything that was going. This particular child, explained Igor, had been a bone of contention between two amorous Sikhs, who used the ambulance train at night for their nefarious purposes. He needed to be rescued.

Gwen, practical as always, wanted to know what would happen to the boy when we all returned home. Jim Hennessy said he would consult Havildar Husain, who was summoned forthwith. Igor Anrep called the boy, who appeared before us, his clothes in rags, his hair unkempt; yet there was no mistaking the bright intelligence of his expression or his eagerness to please. The havildar, after hearing the story, assured us that a job would eventually be found for Noor Din, first on the river steamers and then in the Indian navy – if he proved to be satisfactory and we would speak for him. He sent one of his henchmen to the Red Cross stores for the smallest sets of pyjamas he could find, which, after minor alterations, provided the budding batman with two smart green and white outfits. The kindly havildar, proud to share in the magnanimity of his sahibs, found him somewhere to sleep on deck, saw that he had a good meal and directed him to make himself useful as junior batman to Captain Hennessy.

Before we sailed for Dacca we took on board ten British soldiers, all of them with wounds under their plaster casts, who were bound for the 17th British General Hospital to undergo surgery. Later one of them began to haemorrhage under his leg plaster. The master was informed of the emergency and took his ship down the river faster than he had ever done in his life, reaching Dacca quayside at the same time as the ambulances that had been sent to carry the men to hospital. Jim Hennessy remarked ruefully that there were no plaster-shears on the equipment list and that he was going to the Dacca supply depot to rectify the omission right away. Gwen and I went with him.

The building was by the river and was absolutely overrun with cats, mostly tabbies, but amongst them was a magnificent snow-white female, heavily in kitten, who approached us in a friendly manner. The officer in charge said that the place was ravaged by rats and that the cats were encouraged to multiply. I asked him if, when the white cat had kittens, he would keep one for me, which he agreed to do. A fledgeling cormorant which I had kept in my cabin had lately died of a surfeit of mashed sardines – no one could be persuaded to catch fish from the river for it. A cat would be a much more suitable pet.

That evening we gave a party on deck for Mr McKentish, inviting some of Gwen's friends from the 17th BGH. Rum punch was served, accompanied by delicacies thought up by our old Muslim cook. We drifted in and out of the saloon to admire the ships' lights reflected in the river along the water-front. Mr McKentish made quite a hit with the senior sisters. He stood on deck, leaning in through the saloon window with a large glass of punch in his hand, reminding me irresistibly of Mr Jackson, the amiable toad at Mrs Tittlemouse's party.

Towards the end of the evening Teddy appeared from Comilla. Because he was on sick leave waiting to go home he was

The author (front row, left), Major Quinn RAMC (seated), Captain
Hennessy RAMC (at the back) and VADs at the Lady Mary Herbert Club
swimming pool, Dacca, 1944.

allowed to stay on board for twenty-four hours. He looked
thin and tired, and I was glad that he would have time to recover
and would return to a civil hospital in India. He had threaded
my engagement ring on a gold chain so that I could wear it
round my neck. 'No jewellery to be worn on duty, nurse,' I
reminded Teddy. His face was transfigured by that radiant smile
I remembered from our first encounter. Whatever happened
in the future I would see him as he was then, as he had always
been. I knew that I had changed a great deal in my two-and-a-
half years in India but Teddy had not changed at all. The *Mallard*
sailed early the next evening, leaving him alone on the quay.

Late in October we left Gauhati, bound for Dacca with five
young VADs newly arrived from England aboard. These Red
Cross nurses were lovely responsible girls who would be a tonic
for the troops. Several of those I talked to told me of their inten-
tion to train as QA sisters after the war. They had heard that
the army was to have its own training schools for nurses, who
would become QAs if they reached a certain standard. It seemed

an excellent idea. One of their number, Joan Evers, had already worked with me on two river trips while Gwen was away on leave. Like me, she loved the river and was sorry to return to ward routine.

When we reached Dacca and had handed over our patients, Jim Hennessy and his fellow-Irishman, Major Quinn RAMC of the 17th BGH, took the VADs to the swimming-pool before putting them on the train for Calcutta. It was not only the VADs who had enjoyed the river trip. The British soldiers said it had been like a corner of England with all the pretty girls around after months in the jungle.

On our return to Gauhati Gwen and I were told that, with the reduction in the number of patients in the hospital, we would no longer return to work on the wards between voyages. It was expected that many more sick and wounded Japanese prisoners would be transported by river in the near future, which would necessitate quick turn-arounds for the steamers and their staff.

My last duty at the Gauhati hospital was to 'special', in other words to have in my sole care during the day a dangerously-ill patient. I had just received what was to be my last letter from Major Hugh Sealy, who was to be killed in Italy the following month. He told me he was on his way home for leave. I was delighted to hear that he had completely recovered from his severe head wound and that he was going home to see his wife and family. I remember slipping the letter into my pocket and entering the side ward to take over my new patient from the night sister.

9 November 1944

I am in special charge of Captain Roberts, who is badly burned from an accident he was involved in. It is the worst case of burns I have seen out here, three-quarters of the skin surface being involved. It is so difficult to nurse him under a mosquito net but the flies have to be kept away. His chart tells me that he is forty-one and married. If only a satisfactory treatment for severe burns could be found how much suffering would be avoided and how many lives saved. Now that penicillin has been discovered to deal with infection we badly need a breakthrough for burns.

I can tell from the medical officer's expression that there is nothing we can do. I went to bed as soon as I came off duty as I was so dispirited and tired. I shall read *Totem and Taboo* to keep my mind off Captain Roberts's condition as I'm sure I shan't sleep.

10 November 1944

Captain Roberts died today.

When I returned to the river there had been some changes on the steamers. The *Mallard* had been replaced by the *Sherpa* and Eve Scivea took over from Gwen for one or two trips. Eve was a vivacious brunette with sparkling brown eyes who enjoyed life to the full. Despite her unusual name she had lived in London all her life. I would miss Gwen, though, who could always be relied upon to give me sound 'sisterly' advice.

The end of the monsoon season was a bad time to be out on the river in our flat-bottomed steamer. As the winds changed to a different quarter severe gales rocked the ship alarmingly, while the waves grew dangerously high. We might just as well have been on the open sea. The flooded river was a mile or so wide at times; it washed over the surrounding countryside, causing widespread devastation. In this sort of weather we retired to our cabins at night with life-belts – though the master assured us that we should all drown like rats if the ship over-turned. On several occasions we heard of ferries, overladen with Indians, capsizing in mid-stream. There were few survivors.

We took to fishing in the Brahmaputra but abruptly stopped when we saw a remount unit destroying its maimed horses with a humane killer and letting them drop into the river. Everything is disposed of in the Indian rivers, including human beings who have been murdered or whose relatives cannot afford the wood for the cremation fire. I unwisely bathed in the river at Dibrugarh on one occasion, but shot out of the water when a woman's corpse came floating towards me, her sari-clad body bobbing in the current, her dark hair drifting like seaweed at low tide.

At Goalpara, where we stopped on 5 November for repairs, we fell into conversation with an Indian clerk who had some English blood in him. He lived nearby with his wife and children and asked us if we would come to his house to take tea. As we had time to spare before the ship sailed we accepted his invitation, following him across a field to a simple wood and bamboo dwelling. His Eurasian wife and two children were dressed in European clothes of a type that had gone out of fashion twenty years earlier. We sat and made polite conversation with the husband while the wife prepared tea. A lace cloth was spread on a round table; upon it were placed boiled eggs, bread and butter and a sponge-cake. It was such an unexpectedly genteel occasion. We realised that the man wanted to show us that he knew how English people lived. It was no surprise to us when he mentioned that he did not mix with his Indian neighbours.

Later that day we took on board a complete Chinese hospital unit on its way up river towards the American sector in northeast Assam. Our only contact was by sign language. The fresh-faced British orderly, who was from Newcastle, kept his little dog chained up in his cabin while the visitors were roaming the decks. Havildar Husain had told him that the Chinese looked upon dog meat as a great delicacy, particularly the type of well-nourished puppy that Private Mullen owned. The mongoose soon found its way into the baskets of eggs left in the open by our guests, decimating them in a matter of hours. It required all Captain Hennessy's diplomacy to persuade the Chinese that the crew were not responsible for the thefts and avert a mini-war on our decks.

As night fell we left Goalpara. We let off a few fire-crackers that the crew had managed to find for us in the bazaar in honour

Indian Hospital River Steamer *Sherpa* on the Brahmaputra.

of Bonfire Night. It was not unlike a foggy November evening at home. The squibbs fizzled out in the damp mist, river sounds were muffled, the beat of the ship's engines reduced to a whisper. We seldom passed another vessel on the river but that night a bulky shape materialised out of the fog, mooing dismally; it was the *Kite* bound for Dhubri with its cargo of war-weary souls.

During that winter of 1944–45 we were frequently held up by severe weather. Lack of exercise led us to seek out active occupations. No sooner had we finished the annual painting of the bunks than Jim Hennessy decided that Gwen and I should learn how to handle firearms. The moving scraps of debris on the river were not the easiest of targets. I found the revolver so heavy that I had to rest my arm on the ship's rail and the kick of the rifle bruised my shoulder. Gwen, having stronger wrists, put on a better show but neither of us had any ambition to become markswomen. The theory was that we should be able to defend ourselves or even take our own lives if we were captured by the enemy. We were quite sure that if such an unlikely occasion presented itself we should do neither.

In the winter evenings the staff spent their time working out chess problems, solving crosswords and even playing charades, in which any convalescent officers joined. The hilarity produced by these parlour games caused Havildar Husain to creep along the deck and poke an anxious bespectacled face through the saloon window. It must have been bad enough for him to see his three sahibs engaged in the manual labour of painting bunks, but to hear them enjoying themselves in such an unrestrained manner must have convinced him that we had finally taken leave of our senses.

By Christmas the steamer staff had experienced the disagree-able side of river life: the cold draughty decks where the patients huddled in grey blankets, the shortage of fresh vegetables and the edginess engendered by the presence of prisoners of war, who had started to arrive in a thin trickle. On shore at Gauhati, the elderly General Ranking from 202 Area Command, the local army headquarters, gave a Christmas Eve party. The more abstemious among us went on to a midnight service after touring the wards by the light of an oil lamp and singing carols for the patients.

On New Year's Day 1945 we heard that Colonel Cawthorn was leaving the hospital and that a Colonel Crawford RAMC was taking over. There was a farewell party for our respected,

and by now well-liked colonel, as we understood what responsibilities he had carried at the time of Kohima. I wore my new
red and silver dance frock with very high-heeled scarlet court
shoes from Calcutta. Although I had been suffering from a low
fever for a week or two, I was determined not to miss the dance.
The next day, after laboratory tests, Colonel Ransome diagnosed glandular fever, which was endemic in the area, and I
spent the next few weeks in the American mission hospital. It
had been an unfortunate season for the steamer staff. Captain
Hennessy had twice contracted malaria and was admitted to
the 17th BGH. Two doctors who took over from him went
down in turn with dengue fever.

I certainly caught up with my reading in the hospital as
everyone brought me books – and Charlie Bock good things
to eat. On the day I was discharged, Lily Pons, a soprano from
the United States, sang for us in the open air. She was tiny
physically, which was the reason she was known as the 'Pocket
Soprano', but the volume of her voice was such that it reached
to the outskirts of a crowd of some two thousand people. As
far as I remember she mixed operatic arias with such popular
songs as 'Estrellita' so as to please everybody in the audience.
It was at times such as this that we felt at one with each other.
There was no animosity towards anybody, only a deep longing
for peace and normality once more.

At the end of 1944 it had been decided that the sisters who
worked on the river steamers should have a house of their own
so that they need not return to the hospital between trips. A
pleasant rented bungalow, called Mermaid Villa by the men,
became our headquarters. It had four large bedrooms, a sitting-
room and dining-room whose window spaces were guarded
by heavy wooden shutters, kept open day and night at that
time of the year when there was no need for protection from
the burning sun or monsoon rains. Strong iron bars about six
inches apart – close enough to exclude animal and human
intruders – protected the open windows; only town bungalows
had glass panes.

Mermaid Villa was rather isolated, with patches of jungley
scrub coming close to our small compound. The river ran near
by, with a rough road to Gauhati and the steamer *ghat* beside
it. It was not at all a 'creepy' sort of place. There were always
a few sisters there in the evening, gathered around the piano
to sing, while a cook and bearer saw to it that regular meals
were provided.

One evening soon after Christmas, when there was a little sharpness in the air, I retired to bed with the shutters left open as usual but with a single blanket in case the temperature suddenly dropped in the night. We still used mosquito nets as there were plenty of stray insects from the river mud which would be attracted by the lights in our rooms. In the early hours I woke up with a start. It was pitch dark and there was no sound but I had an uneasy feeling that something was wrong. After listening intently for a minute with my head raised from the pillow, I relaxed and started to turn over in bed, only to discover that I could not move my legs.

My heart started to beat rapidly and my mind went over all the text-book illnesses with symptoms of paralysis. I tried to move my legs again but they refused to respond: they seemed to be paralysed from the knee down. I lay there sweating profusely and entertaining all manner of desperate and gloomy possibilities. After half-an-hour of unrelieved misery I felt a sudden movement at the bottom of the bed; something heavy turned round and resettled itself on my legs. My heart leaped with relief. I was not paralysed after all. My feet must have lost sensation with the weight – but the weight of what? My pulse raced and my mind spun round trying to adapt itself to a new terror. What creature could have crept inside the tucked-in mosquito net without disturbing me? I lay quite still, hardly daring to breathe, remembering those stories told to us in childhood of people whose hair turned white from fear.

Half-conscious, I suddenly heard a chirruping sound and then the weight disappeared from my feet, leaving them still numbed. I fixed my eyes on the window space hoping to see whatever animal it might be, but although the dawn light etched every bar against the sky nothing passed through.

I got up shakily, rubbed my legs to restore the circulation and searched the room. There was no sign of the night visitor, except that the mosquito net had been pulled out from under the mattress at the end of the bed. I went over to the mirror to see if my hair had turned white. It hadn't.

When Abdul Khan, the bearer, came in with my morning tea I told him what had happened. I asked him to poke along the rafters in case a snake was lurking in the roof. Though he found nothing, I knew that even a large python could have escaped through a hole in the thatch. I was glad to get away from the bungalow to the steamer that day, only returning to Mermaid Villa with the firm proviso that I should never have to inhabit that sinister room again.

Late in February we carried a full shipload of West Africans with their British major, whose name I did not record. I believe his men were Chindits of the 81st (West African) Division. I had always imagined that Africans were happy friendly people who sang together at every opportunity – but perhaps I had seen too many films. These men, even allowing for their illnesses, were sullen, silent and grey-faced with cold. I was reminded of what happens to a tropical fish when it is removed from its natural environment. Its sparkle and colour fades to a neutral shade; it is no longer the same darting eager Ariel of the marine world. So it was with these Africans. They were out of their depth, in whatever conditions they had come from.

The major told me that the Indians and Africans did not get on well together, each group considering itself superior to the other. The Africans signed on for a definite time and were liable to become very fractious if they were not allowed home at the end of their term of service. It appeared that their wives put a good deal of pressure on them to return at the appointed time, using methods known only to the African women themselves. I could not help feeling a little sympathy for those crafty wives. This was the only time we carried Africans on our steamer. I heard from a QA sister who had worked at the 56th Indian General Hospital that most of them were based at Chittagong.

Once our African patients had disembarked, the *Sherpa* sailed to Daulkandi and Sanitura for repairs and maintenance, the master promising to be back on the Sirajganj *ghat* by nightfall. We had made the acquaintance of Colonel O'Neill, CO of the 67th Indian General Hospital, a few months earlier when we brought him down the river as a patient. Since then we had had a standing invitation to visit his hospital if ever we had time to spare at Sirajganj. He was a most original Irishman, who could be trusted to make himself at home in whatever part of the world he happened to be. He had organised a vegetable garden, kept poultry and reared pigs for the benefit of his staff and patients. Perhaps the fact that our own medical officer was an Irishman had something to do with the gifts of new-laid eggs, tomatoes and fresh lettuces (well 'pinkied' in a solution of permanganate of potash, which was supposed to kill all known germs). Occasionally we received some fine streaky bacon from the pigs – the only pork we dare eat in India because of the danger of worm infestation.

It was well worth the eight-mile drive in a dusty ambulance 173 to be hospitably entertained by the colonel to cool drinks on the veranda, shown round his 'estate' and allowed to look into his fine airy bedroom, where we noticed that his reading matter was not *Tropical Diseases of the Indian Subcontinent* but *Alice in Wonderland*. Shortly after this visit Colonel O'Neill became ill and we never saw him again. He was approaching retirement and, despite his lively mind and energetic bearing, India was beginning to take its toll of his physical health.

Captain Anrep joined us on 11 April for the voyage to Dhubri. In his arms was the kitten that I had asked for at the Dacca supply depot. We all came on deck to inspect the little creature, which was six months old and pale grey with a ginger plume of a tail. He seemed too infested with worms and fleas to grow into a self-respecting cat that would keep mice – let alone rats – at bay. Igor Anrep said that the staff from the last steamer that had put into Sirajganj from Dacca had handed him over. We bathed the kitten in a weak antiseptic solution, then in soap flakes, drying him on deck in the warm sun. When we brushed him he turned into a fluffy ball of snow-white fur. The Indian orderlies and young Noor Din treated him like a prince, feeding him on scraps of chicken and fish from which the bones had been removed. Noor Din, such a serious little batman most of the time, became a child again when he played with the kitten. I was still learning Urdu and, as I could not remember the word for 'whatever', I repeated it over and over again, '*Jokuch, jokuch.*' Every time I said it the kitten ran to me, so we christened him 'Joe Kutch'.

None of us realised as we anchored at Gauhati with Joe Kutch perched inquisitively on the ship's rail that it was the last time the *Sherpa* would pick up patients there. The small town and the hospital were full of rumours of the 'cessation of hostilities', as the announcer on the sisters' mess wireless described the approaching end of the war in Europe. Soldiers were everywhere, some handling round copies of *SEAC*, the forces' newspaper, others organising the opening of the YMCA Club for British other ranks. The Garrison Theatre posters advertised the coming of an ENSA concert party. Charlie Bock appeared with the photos he had taken of a dance at US army headquarters, plus the last consignment of orange juice and cigarettes that he would ever present me with.

With the fighting now mainly in central and lower Burma, Gauhati received fewer casualties. Dacca was chosen as the new river steamer headquarters as it was near Daulkandi, now to

Joe Kutch the cat on the foredeck of the *Sherpa*, 1945.

be the busiest reception port on the river. The *Sherpa* sailed
with Major Mayne on board, who was due for repatriation and
was on his way to Calcutta. Dorothy Baker, who had been
awarded the Royal Red Cross in February, a decoration that
was first presented to Florence Nightingale by Queen Victoria
in 1883, came with us to Dacca to discuss with the Principal
Matron the purchase of a sister's mess there. Gwen was back
with us once more, the life and soul of the party, assuring us
that victory in Europe would be announced at any moment.
On a more sombre note, Major Mayne told us of the atrocities
that had taken place in German-occupied territory. No one
wanted to believe him.

We reached Dacca early on a Monday morning. Mr McKentish came on board followed by his *khitmagar*, who was carrying
a heavy wireless so that we would be able to listen to the news
on and off all day. In the evening as we all gathered together
on deck we were rewarded by the sound of a newsreader's voice
announcing that the war in Europe was over at last.

British and American nursing sisters at a United States forces dance, Gauhati, 1945. Second row: third and fourth from left, Dorothy Baker, Vicky Udall; third row: second from left, Eve Scivea.

8 May 1945

Major Mayne, Dorothy Baker, Captain Hennessy, Mr McKentish and I sat round the wireless to hear the King's speech at 1.30pm and Winston Churchill's address to the nation at 7.30pm. We had lunch on deck, rather guiltily drinking a bottle of champagne from the Red Cross stores. Gwen has gone off to her friends at the 17th BGH to celebrate.

Next day there was a dance for the forces at the Lady Mary Herbert Club in Dacca, which was swamped by the number of people who tried to get on to the dance floor. Many of the men seemed to be drunk and the military police were very much in evidence. The soldiers did not seem so much to be celebrating as wishing they were back home in Trafalgar Square with the Japanese war over too.

Two days later there was a Victory Ball for officers, at which the Americans were present in force. As usual when there were too few women and too much drink there were several minor punch-ups between the British and Americans but nothing requiring the intervention of the bearers, who had a quick way of stopping a fight. They would seize the nearest chair and throw it towards the trouble spot. It cleared the hall like magic. There was a band which played 'Paper Doll', 'Moonlight Becomes You' and 'Besame Mucho' for the British, and 'Moonlight Serenade' and 'The Blue of Evening', I think it was called, for the Americans and the women; but the men preferred 'In the Mood', which was brisk and lively.

Towards midnight everyone quietened down, the lights were lowered, couples danced cheek to cheek and a crooner sang Vera Lynn's 'I'll Be Seeing You' very softly. The dancers gradually joined in until all the people in the hall were singing together as quietly as they could. It was very moving and unexpected – even 'Auld Lang Syne' at the end was an anti-climax. The leader of the band had caught the mood of the evening perfectly and everyone dispersed peacefully into the warm night.

In the short space between the two celebration dances we went to pick up sixty Japanese prisoners of war at Daulkandi, many of them wounded. Everyone on board was filled with curiosity about these soldiers, who were travelling with their officers for the first time, thus making some form of communication possible.

On this occasion our steamer was the *Kite*, which had no bunks on board; the orderlies had to place the stretchers close together in rows along the decks. Gwen and I worked along the lines of patients, reading their case histories so that we could report anything of interest to Captain Hennessy. To our relief there was an ambulant Japanese doctor who spoke some English leaning on the rail watching the proceedings with two other officers. They did not look like the pictures we had seen of Japanese soldiers. Two of them were tall and quite good-looking even by European standards. We asked the doctor why one of his fellow-officers refused to answer our questions when he patently understood what we were saying. He informed us in a matter-of-fact way that the unfortunate man had cut out his tongue under the mistaken impression that when he was taken prisoner the enemy would torture him to obtain information.

While I was in the middle of serving the evening meal of curry and rice from the canteen an Indian orderly drew my attention to one of the prisoners. He was lying very still with his rice untouched by his side. I was alarmed to find that a large wound in the centre of his chest was bleeding profusely. His livid face and almost imperceptible heartbeat bore witness to his critical condition. On examining the wound, Captain Hennessy found that the injury was such that urgent operating-room treatment was required – yet here we were a day's voyage from the nearest hospital with little more than first aid equipment on board. Suddenly the doctor remembered the blood plasma. Several weeks earlier a few bottles of the new preparation with its apparatus had been given to us. We had never had cause to use them and were inclined to look on them with suspicion, being accustomed to bottles of good red blood and the old method of blood grouping.

Within a few minutes a section of the deck was screened off, a bed prepared and the dying man placed on it. By 8pm the fluid-restoring plasma drip was flowing into his veins. We arranged to take four-hourly watches during the night, Gwen Hallett until midnight, the doctor until 4am and myself until dawn. We went to bed feeling rather hopeless about the patient, who was still bleeding, but we were too tired to do anything but sleep. Four o'clock came all too soon and I dressed wearily in the unaccustomed silence of early dawn. As I went on deck Captain Hennessy greeted me with a tired but triumphant smile. The patient's wound had stopped bleeding, his pulse rate had improved and he was sleeping peacefully.

For the next two hours all was still. From my chair by the patient's bed I could see the lines of stretchers along the deck, so close to each other in their grey-blanketed anonymity that it was difficult to approach them. The air grew colder. As I rose to put more blankets on the bed I noticed the dim moving outline of the river bank, misty in the early light. I wondered about the sick man. He was very young, with a delicate worn face. Where did he live? Had he a mother waiting for him? What was his occupation? It struck me forcibly that never once during the whole emergency had the thought entered my head that this man was an enemy. He was just another patient to us, for whose life we fought. Whether he was friend or foe, Buddhist or Christian, dark-skinned or fair, it made not the slightest difference to our devotion or to our joy on his recovery.

I left him for a moment to walk down the lines of patients to check that all was well. When I returned he was awake, blinking at me nervously with dark almond-shaped eyes. I peeled some juicy lychees, feeding him with them one by one as he opened his mouth, like a child, for more. Then to my surprise he nodded at the fruit, saying in English 'What name?' I told him and added with a smile, 'Chinese fruit!' By now it was daylight and the sounds of the morning prayers rose from the lower deck, the cock crew, the goats bleated and the patients began to stir.

The Japanese doctor peered hesitatingly round the screen, watching the young soldier eating the fruit. He bowed once or twice, stepped forward and made a speech. He thanked the honoured ladies and doctor for preserving the life of this humble soldier. 'Yesterday,' he informed me, 'soldiers all say you take this man away to make an end of him. But I say not so. Now I tell them you have made him well. Three months and war will finish. We have not medical supplies. Thank you honoured lady.' Bowing once more, he withdrew.

A few hours later our patients were transferred to the ambulance train at Sirajganj bound for the 67th IGH. Four orderlies carried our special patient off the ship; as they crossed the gangplank we saw a thin arm raised in farewell. What the Japanese doctor foretold proved true for the war in South East Asia ended in exactly three months.

The fact that we were carrying large groups of prisoners to India was an indication that the tide of war in Burma was flowing steadily in our favour. The cages on the deck were now used not so much to keep patients in as to keep other people out. Frequently Gurkha convalescents travelled alongside the Japanese prisoners. They would stand outside the cage with their kukris raised threateningly as the Japanese soldiers huddled in a corner of the strong-room trying to eat a meal. 'When we prisoners,' shouted the Gurkhas, 'you starve us! When you prisoners, you eat our rice!'

They would act a realistic pantomime of throat-cutting, rattling the bars of the cage in a most alarming manner. After I had intervened once or twice I had to threaten the Gurkhas that if they did it again I would put them in the cage and let the Japanese out. They roared with laughter in a thoroughly good-humoured way, at last leaving the wretched prisoners alone.

I had hardly settled into the new sisters' mess at Dacca when

TO   SISTER A.NOBLET Q.A.I.M.N.S.

SHERPA.

With the compliments of I.A.M.C. Personnel of I.H.R.S.

We all staff feeling sorry for your transfer.

As we can say boldly that your treatment with us just like SISTER (not as per designation).

Therefore we request to God for your health,happines and future prospects.

Dated 16/6/45.

S.I.Husain.
Q.M.Havildar. IAMC.
I.H.R.S. SHERPA.
on behalf of Personnel.

Letter from Havildar Husain to the author on her transfer from the Indian Hospital River Steamers, 16 June 1945.

Dorothy Baker broke the news that I had been posted to the CMH, Dibrugarh. Until I decided what to do about him I handed over Joe Kutch to Joyce Freeman, a sister from Oxfordshire who was to take my place. Old friendships were severed. I would miss Gwen Hallett, Eve Scivea and Doris Oliver.

12 June 1945

I am sure I shall look back to this time on the river as one of the happiest periods in my life. Because we have been taking servicemen away from the battlefield knowing that they would never have to return to jungle warfare there has been a feeling of optimism in the air – I have found the convergence of so many nationalities on one small river boat exhilarating, breaking down my stereotypes of how certain races look and behave.

I do not suppose I shall ever again pick marigolds at Dhubri or gaze upon my enchanted island under the moon. Tomorrow I must stand on the quay to watch our beloved

Sherpa fade into the mists of time, or at least into other people's lives. Good luck to them whoever they may be.

Now that I was moving to a posting that would almost certainly be my last in India it was time to take stock of my situation. First of all I thought of my father and how, despite the antagonism I had felt about his plans for me, my life was shaping in a satisfactory way with regard to occupation and experience. There was nothing wrong with my reactions towards my patients either; I felt moved by their suffering; I mourned bitterly at their too-early deaths; I cared for them as a mother cares for her children. But in the context of my own emotional life I felt a complete stranger. There was always the avoidance of commitment, the fear of being in the power of someone other than myself, no matter how loving the motives or how generous the conditions.

Teddy was on his way back from Canada and I would have to make up my mind whether or not I should marry him. He was a very dear friend and I felt safe and relaxed with him – a year or so earlier I would have married him with no hesitation had the war been over. But something had happened during that year which had made me realise how truly ignorant I was about my emotions and how unsuitable a candidate for matrimony I was turning out to be. Contrary to all my resolutions and expectations I had fallen in love again.

6 · End of an Era

It was with a heavy heart that I left the city of Dacca to catch the midnight train for Parbatipur *en route* for Dibrugarh in the north-east corner of Assam. I consoled myself with the thought that I would still be by the river though over two hundred miles up the Brahmaputra from Gauhati. Two members of the Women's Auxiliary Service (Burma) shared the compartment with me. These invaluable volunteers were encountered wherever there was organisational or supply work to be done in Assam. They drove their vans close up to the Burma borders, bringing tea and sandwiches to the troops. Many of them were planters' wives who had helped to cope with the flood of refugees leaving Burma in 1942.

Before the train started, a railway employee carried in a metal basket containing a huge block of ice, which melted away gradually during the night leaving a pool of water washing about on the floor. A British corporal in the next compartment was detailed by the RTO, who was to be found on every railway station used by army personnel, to take care of us until we reached Parbatipur, his chief duty being to see that we were supplied with a tray of tea and toast in the morning brought by a bearer from the station restaurant.

Two days' travel took us across the Brahmaputra and on to the Assam mail train for the night. The three of us slept soundly, unconscious of passing the hill country of Nagaland on our right, with its railhead at Lumding, and the Manipur Road station for Dimapur further along the track. I regretted not being awake as I very much wanted to see this area, which was not far from Kohima and Imphal where so many of my patients had become casualties, no doubt travelling to hospital by this very railway. Looking at the map I saw that we were only a hundred miles from Silchar, the site of the 124th Indian General Hospital which Teddy had taken over in time for the campaign.

The early morning of 19 June found us sitting on our trunks

at Tinsukia while the boyish RTO, Lieutenant Graham, obviously cheered by the sight of three young women, did his utmost to find transport for us. Nothing happened for an hour or two, then along came – not a knight in shining armour exactly – but an American GI named Gallagher driving a huge truck. Unruly locks of hair stuck out from under his peaked cap. As he was passing the gates of the Dibrugarh hospital he offered to give me a lift.

After taking leave of the friendly Women's Auxiliary Service ladies, I hoisted myself into the cab. Away we went at a spanking pace through the green river valley towards the Brahmaputra. Gallagher indicated the direction of Lhasa, the capital of Tibet, four hundred miles to the north-west as the crow flies. He jerked his head towards the north-east where China, partly occupied by the Japanese, was only two hundred miles away. Geographically, Dibrugarh appeared to be a most exciting corner of Assam, wilder and lonelier than Gauhati. It was here that the waters of the Tsang-po in the Himalayan foothills changed into the stripling Brahmaputra, which gradually broadened out enough to take river steamers on its flood.

When I had become accustomed to the roar of the truck, I asked Gallagher what his particular job was. He explained that he carried materials for a road being built through enemy-infested country to China. This would reopen a supply route that had been closed at the time of the invasion of Burma by the Japanese. He added that the Nips did not like what he was doing at all and often took pot-shots at him from the jungle.

Refusing my companion's offer of chewing gum but accepting some 'candy' I described life on a hospital steamer, mentioning that I had had to leave my cat behind as it was impossible to bring him on such a complicated journey. Before he dropped me off at the hospital gate Gallagher asked me the names of the places the steamer docked at. Then he drove back along the road, his great unwieldy vehicle rocking into all the ruts. I watched him until he was out of sight. Leaving my steel trunk, bedding roll and travelling bag for the servants to deal with, I walked towards the sisters' mess. The harassed-looking, pre-occupied matron informed me that I was a welcome sight as there was a severe staff shortage. Would I please unpack, have lunch and be ready for duty at 3pm. My room was a wood-framed hut with basket-weave walls and a thatched roof that looked as though it might harbour snakes. Out came my camp bed, tent-pole strap and the rest of the camping equipment.

Dakota C47s over Assam.

I quickly changed my travel-stained khaki drill and returned to the mess.

As matron accompanied me across the compound to my wards, two *bashas* with twenty beds each, she said, 'I hope your French is adequate. These are Foreign Legion soldiers.' I did not know what to expect. Having read books such as *Beau Geste* and seen films about the harshness of the officers and the toughness of the men, I hesitated on the threshold of the first *basha* after matron had gone, unwilling to leave the sunlit compound for the shadowy interior. I thought to myself, 'I'm British. I refuse to be intimidated by a pack of Frenchmen!' and stepped inside, doing my best to look like a combination of Florence Nightingale and Edith Cavell.

My fears were unfounded. Those Frenchmen were the gentlest and politest soldiers I had ever come across. They were lying on their beds with their boots off but they rose up as a body when I entered, except for a few very sick men. '*Bonjour messieurs, asseyez-vous,*' I said firmly, going quickly from bed to bed to pick out those who needed urgent care. One of the older soldiers was too weak with amoebic dysentery to lift a mug or wash himself in the bowl provided by the orderly. How well I remembered my own feelings during my bout of infective jaundice. When I tried to help him wash he protested that he must manage for himself, trying hard to squeeze the sponge, but he did not have the strength and the helpless tears poured down his lined face. Most of these strange men did not seem to have illnesses as such but to have come through some appalling test of endurance which had left them drained of vitality.

The next day two Englishmen amongst them were pointed out to me. They sat apart in their shabby, sand-coloured uniforms, having very little to do with the others. When I enquired where they came from in Great Britain their young faces grew mutinous and I presumed they had something to hide. I left them in peace, contenting myself with communicating in schoolgirl French with the more friendly legionnaires.

Three months earlier, they told me, the Japanese, who had been given control of French Indo-China by the Vichy French, demanded that the Legion should hand in their weapons and be interned. Thousands of them rebelled. Many were punished; others escaped in their hundreds to Allied China through five hundred miles of jungle, harried by the Japanese. So far as I could make out, they were airlifted out from Yunan Province to Assam.

For several days the wards were so full that all off-duty was cancelled, causing us sisters to wilt in the increasing heat. Henry and Thomas (surnames I believe), who were liaison officers at the Foreign Legion camp nearby, came to arrange for the transfer of all the recovered men back to their billets. They were not allowed to discuss Legion affairs, though they did divulge the information that the sisters in my repatriation group, 'Python 29', would be starting for home in three months' time. This made me realise that Captains Henry and Thomas had more access to intelligence than the rest of us. It struck me that the Foreign Legion refugees, who had been in Vichy-orientated Indo-China for so long, were in an ambivalent position as far as the Allies were concerned. Their objections to being disarmed and segregated by the Japanese were perhaps an indication of hereditary pride in their service rather than a deep-felt desire to join General de Gaulle's Free French forces. Henry and Thomas, I decided, must be British intelligence officers.

My suspicions were confirmed when I observed the behaviour of the six French Foreign Legion officers in the private ward. What a contrast they were to their men. They were offhand and disgruntled, whispering together continually with set angry faces. They were unable to speak a civil word to anyone, least of all to an English sister whose command of the French tongue was abysmal. Did they, I wondered, think this was a ruse so that I could listen to their conversation and report back to British intelligence?

When the wards became less crowded and we were able to take some time off I visited the local bazaar with Vicky Udall, newly returned from leave and acting as matron. There was the usual thin line of booths with only one well-stocked shop, where I was able to purchase an electric immersion heater for making tea in a jug. To my astonishment, in the same emporium we came across some Elizabeth Arden cosmetics – powder and lipstick – which we bought up for the sisters and VADs. There were few delights out in the wilds to equal the opening of a new box of fragrant-smelling face powder when one had been reduced to scraping the last scraps from the edges of a compact. The only comparable pleasure was to wash one's hair with a newly-discovered bottle of Drene shampoo – such a delight after soap shampoos, which tended to leave the hair slightly sticky.

Several times another sister and I were invited out to dinner at the Foreign Legion camp, discovering Henry and Thomas

187

to be highly articulate, well-read men in their middle twenties, Henry being of Gallic appearance with a meticulous French accent and Thomas of Welsh extraction. Thomas revealed a penchant for catching the literary quotations thrown at him and placing them neatly in context. After a few weeks all the mystery men from the Foreign Legion camp were spirited away.

One evening I came off duty to find a weary and bedraggled Joe Kutch waiting for me outside my room. At first I thought I was dreaming, but he came up to rub himself against my legs as though we had never been parted. The bearer, Abdullah, came out smiling to tell me that an American sahib in a big truck had brought him. 'Gallagher!' I exclaimed. 'Galga,' agreed the bearer, putting down a saucer of milk for the thirsty cat.

The young GI had succeeded in taking his truck on a round journey of several hundred miles (on official business, I presumed), collected Joe Kutch from Jim Hennessy, which must have taken some persuasion, and kept him fed and watered. I never saw Gallagher to thank him personally for his altruistic action but I wrote a letter addressed simply 'Gallagher' and sent it to his unit. I hope he received it.

Towards the end of June the rains turned my *basha* into a damp and dismal place. Unwelcome nocturnal creatures were washed out of bathroom drains into the open gurgling gullies. I was asked to prepare a side ward for the only case of poliomyelitis I came across in India. Corporal England had been serving with a REME unit some miles away and had developed a high fever with breathing difficulties which was diagnosed as that paralysing disease. His friends in the unit fabricated a breathing machine with an attachment round the chest connected to a hand pump. They sent a signal to our hospital asking us to prepare a respirator, if we had one, adding that they would bring the patient to us by van as soon as they could.

After a frenzied search an ancient and battered 'iron lung' was found mouldering away in a storeroom. When the REME officers and men arrived on 25 June, having taken turns to pump the homemade respirator throughout the journey, they checked our machine, only to discover something wrong with the circuit. The engineers overhauled the respirator ready for the next operation, which was a critical one. They had to stop pumping the first machine, slide Corporal England into the 'iron lung', close the lid and adjust the sponge-rubber flange round his neck to form a seal, before switching on the breathing apparatus.

All this they did admirably with the help of the nursing staff and the apparatus took over the corporal's breathing almost at once. It was an exceedingly stressful situation for all concerned, particularly for the patient, who was completely conscious and well aware that his life was at stake.

The following day Corporal England seemed a little better, so much so that I was able to feed him and hold a conversation with him in his coffin-like respirator. We talked about Wales, his own country, and I told him how the rounded hills of the Welsh Marches as you approach from Hereford and Shropshire filled me with a sense of excitement as though a strange ancient world was welcoming me. The Assam hills, he observed, were harsher, more virile, like the bristly chin of a man who hasn't shaved for days. We laughed together at his poetic Celtic metaphor so aptly derived from the three-day growth of beard on his own chin.

The respirator had a mirror attachment which I swivelled round to give him a view of the distant uplands. I thought I knew what was in his mind as he lay there helpless: that he might never set eyes on his native hills again, nor on the chimneys and docks of Cardiff, his home town.

Major McQuine came to see him, as did two REME officers, who were standing by in case the respirator needed attention. We were all quite hopeful about our patient, happy as people are when they have snatched a human being from the jaws of death. When I returned to my *basha* that evening I found Joe Kutch waiting for me as usual. He was very sorry for himself, having had a fight in the drain with a rat, which bit him on the paw. He had, however, killed the rat, thoughtfully placing it on my pillow.

27 June 1945

Corporal England is dead. There was no struggle, he simply stopped breathing, the anxiety and hardship of the journey to the hospital, or the spread of the disease, causing his heart to falter and then stop. He was twenty-five years old. Such a number of people have been involved in his struggle for life that a gloom is cast over the hospital. I feel particularly sorry for the men and officers of the Royal Electrical and

Mechanical Engineers who have put so much of themselves into the effort to save him.

John Leslie England, sleep in peace among the alien hills.

After a fortnight of night duty I was given a few days' leave by matron. In the quiet watches I had read and reread a letter from Teddy who was biding his time in Dacca on his return from Canada, waiting to take over the Campbell Hospital, Calcutta. He asked me to join him there to arrange our wedding.

For the first time in my life I simply did not know what to do. I asked myself if it were possible to love two men at the same time yet in different ways – or did it mean that I loved neither. Perhaps – alarming thought – one went on falling in love one's whole life through, with marriage being a firm commitment between two people to allow their relationship to deepen at leisure and to become less possessive. In that case, did it matter whom one married so long as there was a certain compatibility?

When I fell in love with Teddy I was still at the stage when I believed that, waiting somewhere in the world was the one man I would love for ever to the exclusion of all others. I presumed I had found that man, being confident that my affections would remain exactly the same despite the long separations caused by the war. After I was posted to Gauhati I attended only official functions for a time, living solely for the letters from Teddy that arrived in batches every week or two. Before long I began to feel that I was behaving churlishly when there was such a dearth of females, so I started to accept invitations to parties and picnics, meeting a great many pleasant young doctors and other officers in the process. It was rather like being on the *Monarch of Bermuda* again – that easy cameraderie of a group of friends without any romantic attachments, on my part at least, that lasted for several months.

But then, out of the blue, it came; a most powerful attraction, stronger than anything I could have imagined possible. This could not happen to me, I thought, not to steady, reliable, faithful me. But it had and – what was worse – he was a happily married man. There was no doubt that the attraction was reciprocal and the fact that he was in my immediate circle of friends and colleagues made it my duty to ask for a posting elsewhere – preferably to the front line in the mood I was in. But I hesitated and was lost.

190   I tried desperately to work out what had gone wrong. I loved

Teddy no less dearly but I began to see that he had been something of a father figure, taking all decisions for me, indulging me, making up to me for the years I had been deprived of affection. He was a dozen years older than I was. He fascinated me by his knowledge of life, his wide experience of the Indian subcontinent, his love of music; he was kind, gentle and humorous and would have made a splendid husband.

This second love affair taught me a great deal about myself that I didn't much like. Formerly I had prided myself on being in control of my emotions – cool, efficient, independent – and now this shattering, frightening passion destroyed all my carefully-nurtured self-possession. I began to realise that there were many different ways of loving and many different reasons for it – intellectual attraction, physical attraction, tender pity and a desire for security.

This settled, I accepted the way I felt, decided that I would just have to live with it and managed to get through the year of proximity with the help of one or two friends. I learnt tolerance of other people's love affairs and the importance of physical attraction in relationships, which up till then I had consistently underrated. Because no harm was done to anyone and no vows were broken, the charm and freshness remained for always with neither regrets nor disenchantment as far as I was concerned. I hope it was the same for him.

One bright morning at the end of July, my first day of leave, I boarded a Dakota at Dinjan air base bound for Calcutta. It was a memorable flight because I was allowed to take the controls for a while, gaining a perfect view of the Brahmaputra River basking like a great shining silver serpent in the green ooze, then breaking up into myriads of little scintillating snakes as we approached the delta. Later I buried my nose in a book, pretending to read, but in an agony of indecision as I tried to make up my mind what to do about Teddy. The second lover was still writing regularly to me and my feelings towards him were just as strong – how could I possibly marry this patient and altogether admirable man? I would tell him the whole story of course and he would have to decide what to do.

I argued with myself all the way to the Grand Hotel and I weighed up the pros and cons all night. It would be sensible to marry and have children while I was young; I would be safe and protected for the rest of my life; it would put the final seal on those youthful fantasies and poetic yearnings which had already been sternly disciplined during my training. But when

Teddy knocked on the door and entered my room I knew what my decision was.

There he stood, tall, thin, tanned and fit after the sea voyage, regarding me in a questioning way before moving forward with the affectionate indulgent smile that I remembered so well. We sat on the bed while I told him what had happened, ending by slipping off my engagement ring and closing his hand round it. He asked me to come out to Prince's Restaurant for dinner with him, hoping to make me change my mind, but I thought it better we should separate for the present, afraid of being shaken in my resolution.

This was no noble renunciation on my part; it was just that I could not bear our two-and-a-half years of perfect friendship to peter out in a half-hearted marriage.

My only wish when I found myself alone in Calcutta with the broken engagement behind me was to get back to work in Dibrugarh as soon as possible, but in this I was to be frustrated. On the first day I missed the plane through not having a colonel's signature on my pass. Back I went to the Grand Hotel for another night. I called at the travel bureau to collect the necessary signature and reported to Dum-Dum next morning. This time the plane had damaged its wing and could not fly. I returned in the oppressive monsoon heat to a hostel as there was no room at the Grand. After a sleepless night, with a noisy punkah clicking overhead accompanied by the infuriating whine of a mosquito trapped in the mosquito net, I took a taxi to the airfield. At last we became airborne, actually flying for ten minutes before the co-pilot put his head into the cabin to say, 'Something's wrong. We shall have to go back to Dum-Dum.' He added half-playfully, 'If we hadn't got you on board, sister, we would have risked it.'

I felt like shouting, 'Go on! Risk it! I can't face Calcutta for the fourth time!' but I knew it would be no use. Those poor old battered Dakotas had to be taken care of, even pampered, as they were all we had. The co-pilot's remark about my presence was his way of making a virtue out of necessity. We turned back to Calcutta.

I went straight to the travel bureau feeling slightly hysterical. 'Look,' I said to the clerk, a Bengali official with a plump face and large spectacles. 'I just have to get back to Dibrugarh. No one will believe that I missed the plane for the fourth time. It's getting beyond a joke.'

'What's the problem, sister?' I spun round to face two

gorgeously apparelled army officers – one a major-general, the other a brigadier. I explained my predicament, adding that I did not want to let matron down as she had been generous in giving me a few days' compassionate leave. 'Don't worry,' said the white-haired, moustached general, 'I'll have a signal sent to Dibrugarh L of C headquarters and they will inform matron of the delay.' I could see that they were amused at my earnestness. The general went over to speak to the clerk. The middle-aged, twinkling-eyed brigadier explained, 'That's Major-General Thompson, head of medical services in Assam. I'm seeing him off to Comilla. By the way, as you must be on your own in Calcutta would you be willing to join me for dinner at the Grand?'

I accepted with relief, not wishing to spend another miserable evening alone in the hostel thinking of Teddy and wondering if I had done the right thing by him after all. It was a delightful occasion, which for a while lifted me out of my mood of depression. Both Brigadier Howard and the officer he had brought with him wanted to know my impressions of the army authorities in India and, in particular, what the QAs thought of the RAMC. I told them that we had always found the authorities to be protective and accommodating towards us and cited the case of the Sikh ambulance driver. The medical officers and sisters worked much more as a team than they did in the hospitals at home. The unquestioning reverent obedience to doctors that had been instilled into us when we were training had changed to an easy comradeship that made life pleasanter and more productive of ideas for the patients' welfare. I hoped that my views would be reported back to General Thompson.

While I was combing my hair and renewing my lipstick in the cloakroom half-way through the evening, who should enter but Mary King, back at the BMH, Calcutta, once more. She looked a different person from the retiring, self-effacing beauty with the detached expression I remembered; her sleepy blue eyes were wide and alert, and she greeted me with an enthusiasm I had never known before. It did not take me long to spot the cause of the transformation. I saw that she was wearing a diamond ring on her left hand. She told me that she had just become engaged and was at the Grand with her fiancé to celebrate. I was so pleased that I gave her a hug and a kiss, a thing I would never have dared to do in the past.

I had to rise early for my plane and I was dropped off at the hostel by Brigadier Howard, who made sure that there was a taxi outside by 8 o'clock the following morning to take me to Dum-Dum.

6 August 1945

The plane left on time, piloted by Squadron-Leader Scragg with Flying Officer Arnold as co-pilot. It was a perfect flight, without incident. As I was the only passenger on this regular run from Calcutta I was allowed into the cockpit to see the dreadful river-floods caused by the heavy monsoon rains. We dipped down low enough to distinguish the great trees and bamboo huts swept along by the turbulent tide. Sheets of water several miles wide spread out on either side with islands of raised terrain dotted about amongst them. I noted with nostalgic interest the river steamers hugging the banks higher up the river, looking like children's toys in the waste of water. I realised what easy targets they would have made if the Japanese had broken through to Gauhati and wondered if one of the steamers was the dear old *Sherpa*.

When I arrived back at the hospital nothing was said to me about my late return. Major-General Thompson had been as good as his word.

Hardly had I settled into my ward routine, ably assisted by Nurse Dorothy Wylie, a young VAD, than the news came through that the Japanese war was over. It was quite unexpected and took us completely by surprise.

15 August 1945

HEARD JAPANESE WAR ENDED LAST NIGHT.
We all went for a drink to the RAMC officers' mess then on to John Lavender's farewell party.

Major Lavender, a fresh-complexioned, forty-year-old RA officer, whose well-fleshed figure was running to fat, had had the misfortune to pick up mumps. The disease attacked with every disagreeable complication it could muster and John was a shadow of his former self when he reached convalescence. As his stint of service in India was almost over, it was decided that he should be repatriated. Conveniently his farewell party coincided with the end of the war.

Nobody appeared to be particularly excited. Ever since VE-Day we had known that it was only a matter of time before men and materials would be released to overcome the enemy in South East Asia. It had ended more quickly than we had expected, that was all. Several days later we heard rumours about a huge bomb being dropped on Hiroshima but this meant little to us at the time.

John Lavender's party was a quiet affair. Nobody wanted to dance. We played some gramophone records, one of which was César Franck's 'Symphonic Variations'. The music, suggesting the huge fall and swell of the ocean – waveless, immense, eternal – the antithesis of human greed and aggression, would have kept me happy for the rest of the evening. Then someone remarked that the piece was too serious for a celebration party and put on a record of a Turkish rondo by Mozart, feverishly martial yet with a plaintive sadness about it. Afterwards we sat talking quietly about the future, trying to imagine what life in England would be like on our return home. Captain John Paxton, a chunky, comical-faced Scot who seemed to spend his time whizzing between his mess and the club on a powerful motor bike, declared that he had voted Labour by postal vote in the 1945 election. Most of the officers present had done the same. The younger men were particularly concerned about opportunities for employment after being freed from anxieties on that score for so long. Army life was a very sheltered one in many respects and several who had been students before joining up would have to fend for themselves for the first time in their lives.

At the end of the evening Sister Frazer from Osmotherly, Yorkshire, who had married in India two years earlier, leaned over and whispered that she had just discovered that she was expecting a baby. It seemed a good augury for the future.

We had to have a Victory Ball of course, though I don't remember there being any great enthusiasm for it. There was a flatness in our emotions; all we wanted to do was to pack up and go home to whatever corner of the Commonwealth we had come from. With the capture of Rangoon in May a war weariness had set in. Our particular job was done and it was time to lower the curtain.

In contrast the wards were happy places, the convalescent soldiers eagerly looking forward to repatriation. They were a cheerful bunch on my ward, forever playing tricks on the orderlies. Sergeant Lowe (I think that was his name) lost his

The author with some of her convalescent patients, Combined Military Hospital, Dibrugarh, Assam, 1945.

false teeth to the rats one night and was never allowed to forget it. He had left them in a mug by his bedside, neglecting to cover them, and they were stolen away to be gnawed at leisure in the rafters. He refused to be photographed without his teeth, which was why he was missing from the snap that was taken of some of the patients outside the convalescent ward.

I was running two wards at that time, one of them being the officers' ward. There was a certain captain, a man of fifty with a boil on his chin, who used to tell a series of vulgar stories while I was doing his dressing, in an attempt to embarrass me in front of the other officers. I responded with icy coldness. When this had no effect on his rhinoceros hide I carefully bound his bandage round and round his mouth to prevent him speaking, tying it securely behind his head with a large safety-pin. I picked up the dressing tray and walked calmly out of the ward, leaving the orderly to attend to him from then on.

As the orderly, who was very hard-worked, was taking over part of my duties, I offered to perform his daily ritual of pouring out a medicinal dose of alcohol for each convalescent officer. All I knew about drinks was from the receiving end: some concoction would be placed in my hand at a party and that was it. I interrupted the patients' enthusiastic conversation about Schnabel's interpretation of Mozart's 21st Piano Concerto to ask them in turn whether they wanted rum, gin or whisky. Then I hesitated. How much was a 'tot', as they called the dose? Following the example of the barman on the *Monarch of Bermuda*, I approached each officer, poised a bottle of his chosen spirit above the glass, and invited him to 'say when'.

It took exactly three days for me to find out my mistake. When I called on matron for further supplies of alcohol as all my bottles were empty she was horrified. 'Good gracious, sister, what on earth have you been doing with it? The next issue is not due for four days.' She peered at me through her spectacles, looking for incipient signs of dipsomania. I explained what my method was, which caused her to set her jaw in a very determined way. 'Very well, sister, those officers who have taken advantage of you shall do without their ration of alcohol until the next issue is due.' She flounced off to deal with the miscreants.

The Victory Ball took place on 17 August at a large hall with a polished wooden floor which was used for army functions. I carefully unwrapped my duck-egg blue evening frock, bought at Dora Smith's of Calcutta, from its tissue-paper nest, placing it on a hanger ready for the festivities. It had to be kept in my steel trunk as long as possible in case the ants ate it. I hoped there wouldn't be rain lest the dress shrink like the one at Asansol, for it was made of crêpe with thin shoulder-straps and a wide swirling skirt cut on the cross that floated out when you were dancing.

I must have been poor company that night as I felt depressed and apathetic. I had been doing a useful absorbing job that was nearly finished; my emotional world was in ruins. I was at my lowest ebb. I remembered little of the dance or of the party of six people I went with. The words of the songs seemed trivial and the tunes we danced to dated and sentimental. The band played a slow foxtrot to the music of a song by Beryl Templeman, an English girl who had a pleasant rather plaintive voice. She was not in the Vera Lynn class but found favour with the servicemen of SEAC. 'Heart of mine, don't run away', we sang as we danced slowly round the floor in the dim light:

'Don't let the stars above hear what you say.
In their spell before
You know how you fell before,
Listen to me heart of mine, don't be fooled once more.'

I recalled how we used to play that record on the river steamers, together with 'I'll See You Again' from *Bitter Sweet* and 'Lover Come Back to Me' from *Blue Moon*, always turning the sound up so that the patients could hear them. Love and loss; 'absence makes the heart grow fonder' – in peace or war it was just the same. Nobody sang about middle-aged, happily-married couples. It seemed odd when you came to think about it.

On the morning after the Victory Ball a letter arrived from my younger sister Winefride who had reached India, having sailed by way of the Suez Canal. She was on her way to the military hospital in Ranchi. Win and I had done the same things in life, she following me into nursing though at a different training school (Blackpool New Victoria Hospital), to Banstead and finally overseas via Anstie Grange in Surrey, where the initial officer training course for QAs was accepting its first recruits from civil hospitals. I immediately put in an application for a week's leave, though I doubted that this would be long enough for us to catch up on all there was to tell each other after a separation of three years and nine months.

Early in September I set out for Calcutta *en route* for Ranchi. The Dakota was thick with dried mud, which obliterated the portholes and encrusted the casing. It looked so decrepit that I doubted whether it would make it to Calcutta. As we settled down on the uncomfortable seats, which were no more than benches running round two sides of the cabin, I became aware of a row of elderly men in crushed khaki with pale weary faces staring blankly into space, their bodies slumped into attitudes of despondency. When I enquired of the man sitting next to me who they were he told me that they were high-ranking British officers who had been taken prisoner in the Far East early in 1942. They had been airlifted out of China having, he thought, originally come from Japan, and were now on their way home via British hospitals in India.

Poor gentlemen! I could have wept for them, they looked so weak and thin. To think that they had been languishing in captivity when they should have spent the last few years playing with their grandchildren and relaxing in the garden or on the golf course. The incident upset me more than many worse things I had come across, filling me with a sense of the utter futility of war.

At Calcutta I caught the crowded train for Ranchi, where, the two RA officers sitting opposite told me, there was a large transit camp for army personnel. For a while I gazed out at the Bengal plain, its fields devoted to the straight bamboo-like jute plants, relieved by coconut, bamboo and banana groves. These changed to paddy-fields with mud-brick and whitewashed settlements as we crossed the Bihar border. One of the officers, Captain Charles Baxter, offered me his map so that I could see where we were making for. Ranchi was situated on the Chota-Nagpur plateau a thousand feet above sea level and about two hundred miles west of Asansol. The area had been used as a training ground for Fourteenth Army jungle fighters, being ideally suited because of the thickly-wooded hills, which were inhabited by aboriginal tribesmen. Captain Baxter appeared to be a very well-informed man; I couldn't help noticing that he was very good-looking too, dark-haired and strongly-built with the quiet self-assurance that so many of our officers in their late twenties and early thirties possessed. His friend was agreeable also but never initiated a conversation, merely filling in the gaps with his shrewd comments.

The two of them helped me with my bag and put me into a taxi on our arrival at Ranchi station before proceeding to the transit camp. I arrived at the British military hospital by four o'clock to find that my sister, who was on night duty, was due to be awakened. I took the tea tray from the bearer, adding an extra cup and saucer, and entered the darkened room, opening the shutters so that the golden afternoon sun flooded in. Winefride awoke to see the sister she had not set eyes on for so long sitting on the bed. We embraced, both talking at once, delighted to find that we looked much the same as when we had parted – except for being more sun-tanned. After the long absence I had become more conscious of my sister's appearance, noticing how attractive she was with her small features and short golden-brown curls. She was finding the Indian climate even more trying than I had, despite the fact that Ranchi was considered to be almost a hill station. It was fortunate that her stay out East would be a great deal shorter than mine.

Winefride came with me the following morning when I made the routine visit to the station office to report my presence in the town. There we found my two acquaintances from the train, who lost no time in inviting us to join them at the Services

Club that evening. Matron gave my sister a late-night pass, making it possible for us to dance until 11pm. Half of the club room was a bar where soldiers were enjoying themselves until quite suddenly a fight broke out over a Eurasian girl. Chairs were hurled across the room by the bearers, the uninvolved males ushered the women out of doors and the manager rang the Military Police. The row subsided as quickly as it had begun and we made our way back into the hall to continue dancing. This sort of set-to was by no means unusual. It was difficult enough for the regular soldiers in India to be deprived of female companionship but for the volunteers and conscripts who were used to a normal social life in England it was very much worse.

After the four of us met for dinner the next night Charles Baxter and his friend were posted away from Ranchi. It had been one of those 'ships that pass in the night' acquaintanceships that so often occur in wartime and post-war conditions. At least we could be fairly sure at this stage that they would not be killed or wounded.

As I was sitting reading in the mess common room after Win had gone to bed for the day, matron came in with a stockily-built senior officer, whose square short-moustached face seemed vaguely familiar. I was sure I had seen it in the pages of *SEAC*. He was a general as far as I could make out from my corner of the room and was doubtless visiting the patients in the hospital. It wasn't until months later that I realised that he was almost certainly General Slim,

Two days later I left Ranchi for Dibrugarh, knowing that Win and I would not be able to meet again until we were both back home. Nevertheless we had survived the war, the Banstead bombs and the voyage to India, to say nothing of all the dangers and diseases so far. Win advised me to take home as much household linen as possible in my bedding-roll as materials were controlled by a system of dockets in England. We said goodbye in her room.

On the train to Calcutta I shared a compartment with two Women's Auxiliary Corps (India) girls, light-skinned Eurasians who lived in Ranchi and were returning to their army office jobs in Calcutta. Large numbers of local British and Eurasian women did their war service in this corps as drivers or stenographers. The door opened at a small station to admit a Government of Burma official, who introduced himself and got into conversation right away. Before we reached our destination he had proposed marriage, leaving me quite dumbfounded. I was hard put to it not to burst out laughing in his face but did not want to hurt his feelings. What curious things people did! I once had a proposal from an Indian bank manager in Dibrugarh when I called at his office to arrange for money to be sent home. When I politely refused he offered me an overdraft which I didn't need.

For the six hundred miles from Calcutta to Dibrugarh I was alone in my coupé, reading James Hilton's *Goodbye Mr Chips* and Louis Blomfield's *The Rains Came* or staring out of the train windows making plans for my life after I returned to England. I would buy a cottage near a country hospital with my hard-earned savings, plus the bonus the army gave you, where I would work as a ward sister and write about India in my spare time. Also I would have a neat little cat like Joe Kutch – and of course a garden where I could grow flowers and vegetables. The scenery outside was changing. I knew I was nearing the end of my journey when I saw that the rough tumuli hills of Nagaland had been replaced by green fields, each holding its resident adjutant stork, huge and heavy-billed, squatting in a corner watching for frogs.

On the following day, 19 September, I was back on the officers' ward once more. There was an invitation from the British other ranks in the area to a dance at the Planters' Club that evening. I was tired after travelling in the heat and then working a long day but it was a point of honour that we females should support any entertainment for the troops as they got little enough as far as we could tell. Nurse Wylie, the rather manic but likeable VAD on my ward, with springy dark hair and winsome face, accompanied me, chatting happily about all the events of the past week. After we were seated in a row on the chairs provided, the men came forward, hair sleeked back with Brylcreem or its Indian equivalent, drill trousers starched as stiffly with rice-water as the dhobi could manage, and asked us politely for a dance. The warrant officers saw to it that every man had the chance of a turn round the room but no drinking was allowed and cigarette smoking was carried on discreetly while the records were being changed. I always felt that these social occasions were just as important as our work on the wards, giving the men something to talk about and dress up for; nor were the benefits one-sided. Most of the servicemen who attended these functions were experts in the art of ballroom dancing, the adroitness of their footwork approaching the virtuosity of Fred Astaire himself.

The day ... ...

<u>PROGRAMME OF GRAMOPHONE RECORDS.</u>

<u>Officers' Club Dibrugarh, Thursday 20 Sept. 1945.</u>

1.	Overture Barber of Seville.	Rossini.	Toscanini & Phil. of N.Y.
2.	Nutcracker Suite.	Tchaikovsky.	Stokowski & Philadelphia.
3.	Air for the G String.	Bach.	Thibaud.
4.	Eine Kleine Nachtmusik.	Mozart.	Walter. & Vienna Phil.
5.	Sonata in C Sharp Minor- Moonlight.	Beethoven.	Backhaus.

INTERVAL for DINNER.

6.	Overture -Fidelio.	Beethoven.	Walter & B.B.C. Symphony.
7.	Concerto No 5 in E Flat Major "Emperor."	do.	Sargent, Schnabel, & Lond Symphony.
8.	Symphony No 7 in A Major.	do.	Toscanini & Phil. of N.Y.

Programme of gramophone records, Officers' Club, Dibrugarh,
20 September 1945.

The officers who accompanied the men were not permitted to dance, being reduced to propping up the small bar. As Dorothy Wylie and I returned to our seats after a lively quickstep, I noticed a lieutenant amongst them whose dark hazel eyes gazed out upon the company with a thoughtful observant expression. He was smoking a pipe and had a pint of beer beside him. Tall, thin and dark-haired, with a pale clear skin, he looked like a young poet. I said half-jokingly, 'There's the man I shall marry,' wondering why I said it. In the three months I had been in Dibrugarh I had never set eyes on him and the chances were that I should never see him again. Dorothy found my declaration to be enough out of character for her to ask me if I were feeling all right, to which I replied, 'Never better.'

The day after the dance was a very hot one. When I finished work I went straight to bed with a book, intending to have a really long sleep. I was just drifting off into oblivion when in bustled Vicky Udall. 'The sisters have been asked to attend a concert of classical music at the Planters' Club,' she said, brushing her long pepper-and-salt hair and winding it up on top of her head. 'I can't find anyone who is free. Be a sport and come with me. I can't go alone.'

'Go away,' I groaned. 'Let me sleep.'

'You simply must come,' she persisted. 'They will be so disappointed. They're putting on a dinner for us too.'

'Go away!'

'You are always complaining that you don't hear enough decent music and now that you have the chance to hear some you turn it down.' She seized the sheet and pulled it off me.

'Very well, I give in, but I shall certainly fall asleep during the concert and disgrace us.' I reached for my khaki-drill bush jacket and slacks, dabbed on powder and lipstick and followed her out like a zombie to the waiting jeep.

At the club a group of six officers were standing round the gramophone sorting out records. One of them was obviously the organiser. It was the lieutenant with the arresting eyes that I had noticed the night before. We were introduced, saying the usual polite things, before the concert began. I most certainly did not fall asleep but the music washed over me in waves and I doubt if I distinguished Beethoven from Bach.

Lieutenant James Bolton worked at the lines of communication sub-area headquarters at Dibrugarh. He was in the Royal Artillery and his parents lived in Sussex. That was the extent of the information I gained from him when we met.

On the officers' ward were two RA captains – Barber and Bamber – the former suffering from an injury to the face, the latter from recurrent malaria. Paul Barber was having to put up with a great deal of pain from his wound and John Bamber in the next bed endeavoured to cheer him up, despite feeling very feverish and unwell on the days when the malaria parasites were coursing through his bloodstream.

Into the ward the following evening, accompanied by an older man, came James Bolton, ostensibly to visit his two sick friends for the first time. The mature captain with him appeared to stand *in loco parentis* to the three younger men. His name was Lindsay Spencer. They worked together under General Ranking, whom I had already come across at Gauhati. It was not long before I heard John Bamber telling his visitors about the deplorable drink-ration incident in which he had played the part of the leading miscreant. I quietly left the ward.

Day after day the four men spent the visiting hours together so that I began to know a great deal about them. They quickly discovered that I could be drawn in their direction if they put on a gramophone record. John Bamber was revealed as a budding lawyer from Manchester, an Oxford graduate with a brilliant future before him. He was a sensitive self-deprecating man, hiding his deep concern about his drinking habits beneath a clowning, devil-may-care exterior. Sadly, having tried marriage as a desperate and dubious remedy, he died in his forties, childless and alone.

Paul Barber I never knew well for he avoided me, resenting perhaps the advent of a woman into what had been an all-male enclave; but Lindsay Spencer was a most tactful, thoughtful and altogether charming man, who saw to it that his co-visitor, James Bolton, should have ample opportunity for discussing the state of health of his two bedridden friends with the ward sister before returning to headquarters. Moreover the now Acting Captain Bolton increasingly appeared at social functions that he had formerly steered clear of and I was at last able to ask him whether or not he was a poet. He had to own up that he was indeed one, though mainly of Greek and Latin verse. I found him painfully shy, a condition he did his best to disguise by a flippant jokey way of talking. He was an only child whose life had been given over to academic pursuits – prep school, Dulwich College, Wadham College, Oxford, where, as a classical scholar, he achieved a Double First. He also won the Chancellor's Prize for Latin Verse. I plucked up enough courage to tell him of my own delight in turning the poetry of Catullus and Ovid into English verse, adding that if a way could be found to introduce females to Latin poetry instead of concentrating on Caesar's *Commentaries* there would be a great many more Latin scholars in the girls' schools of England.

At last the great day came when, after a musical evening, James outmanoeuvred my escort and saw me up to the door of the sisters' mess. 'May I write to you when you go home?' he asked, holding my hand. 'Certainly,' I said. As there were rumours that 'Python 29' would be repatriated shortly I was concerned that I might suddenly disappear without even an opportunity to exchange addresses.

We saw each other every evening for a week, until, after a picnic on the banks of the Brahmaputra to celebrate James's twenty-ninth birthday, he proposed to me late at night in the deserted sitting-room of the sisters' mess. Vicky, coming in late, insisted on opening a bottle of whisky and we drank a toast while Joe Kutch tore the sofa cushions apart in pursuit of an imaginary mouse.

Later in the week James – or Jim as his friends called him – was invited out to a local tea planter's luncheon, where his plump and gossipy host enquired, 'Did you hear about the silly young couple who got engaged after knowing each other only sixteen days?' 'Yes,' spoke up my brand-new fiancé, 'I'm half of it!'

On 10 October, with the wards nearly empty, orders came through for 'Python 29' to stand by in readiness to start for home. I had an hilarious dinner with Jim's friends to celebrate our engagement, now four days old, at which we booked John Bamber as our best man. We discussed a story which we had heard at a function presided over by General Ranking the evening before. An officer at one of the camps in the area had hung his mess-dress trousers over a wooden beam in his *basha* in preparation for the general's party. During the night the termites marched along the beam, ate through the trousers and marched on again. When the officer came to put the trousers on, he found that there were just two threads holding each leg together. He was obliged to attend the function wearing khaki drill slacks with a mess-dress top; a couple of brother officers volunteered to stand in front of him whenever the general looked in his direction.

12 October 1945

Today I started to pack my steel trunk, carefully folding my three evening frocks and wrapping them in tissue-paper. The crisp white broderie-anglaise organdie with its white satin slip showing through, the sleeves puffed, the neck line demurely 'sweetheart' style, takes me back in memory to Asansol, where my first lover, not a dancer himself, watched patiently whilst I whirled round the floor with other men. Dear gentle Teddy, I hope he finds happiness with someone else.

Next for the trunk is the slinky red and silver dress made from a sari, which made me feel very sophisticated as I waltzed through the planters' clubs, officers' messes and steamer decks of Gauhati, Shillong and Dacca in the arms of the man I could never marry. The faint scent of Tosca 4711 rises like a ghost from its silken folds.

Finally I removed from its hanger the duck-egg blue crêpe frock, its colour delicate as the sky after rain. This is the dress that I wore on the night of the Victory Ball at Dibrugarh when I felt at my lowest ebb. Another young man was watching me across the room that evening. It was weeks before we met. He was Captain James Bolton of the thoughtful eyes!

During the past week I had told Jim of my previous engagement and unhappy love affair, knowing that I had finally set my hand to the plough and would never turn back. Before I left Dibrugarh there was something else I had to do. I must write to Teddy, who I knew would care about what happened to me as much as I cared what happened to him. His reply came by return: he was engaged to an American girl. I was content.

Jim was given a few days' leave in which to see me off in Calcutta; Vicky, also on her way home, joined us on the mail train at Tinsukia. The solicitous Lindsay Spencer organised the luggage, his tall, well-built figure towering above the clamouring coolies.

Dorothy Wylie promised to keep in touch, reassuring me about Joe Kutch, who had to be left behind once more. There seemed to be no long-term security for him but Abdullah offered to take care of him when all the sisters and VADs had left. As a reward I let him have my old gramophone, which he had always coveted.

Royal Artillery officers at Durban on their way to the Far East, 1943.
Lieutenant James Bolton is in the back row on the extreme left.

On the last occasion I had stayed in Calcutta I could not escape from it quickly enough but now every minute spent in its noisy streets was precious. After I had finished shopping for household linen and presents for my family, Jim took me to Hamilton's to choose an engagement ring. This elegant jewellers in Park Street was something of an institution in the city. I wore the dainty circle with its three small diamonds at Prince's Restaurant that evening. My three friends from the *Sherpa*, Gwen Hallett, Joyce Freeman and Jim Hennessy, who were waiting in Calcutta for repatriation orders, reacted with delighted surprise. Shrewd Gwen in particular approved of my choice of husband, giving him various pointers about my general management and supervision. She ought to know, she insisted, for she had lived with me long enough to be aware of all my shortcomings. I for my part knew that I had taken on an individual with a profound and complex personality, the exploration of which should keep me happily occupied for the rest of my days.

All too soon the time arrived for Jim and me to take one of those suicidal taxis to Howrah station, where I watched his battle-dressed outline dissolve into the khaki blur of a demobilising army on the move. There were troops everywhere, crowding the trains for the west with one objective in mind – to get a foothold on a ship that would take them home. In the packed compartment of the train as it sped on towards Deolali, a hundred miles north-east of Bombay, I had the comfort of knowing that I was on the way to England, but for Jim there was only the long miserable trek back to Assam.

At Deolali, notorious to generations of British troops as the transit station where you waited for ever for a passage, I came across many old friends and acquaintances. Marty Adair and Monica Lamb arrived from Comilla; Dick Burton from 'Angela's Own' battery proudly escorted his new wife, who was also a QA sister; then Joyce Freeman and Ann Frazer appeared, but there was no sign of Doris Oliver and Gwen. I was not surprised to hear that Mary McNally had been married in April.

Conditions, at least for those with commissions, were really quite good at the camp, despite the large numbers of people who had to be fed, housed and kept reasonably content while awaiting repatriation. There was an outdoor swimming-pool surrounded by grass (a rarity in India) where we could sunbathe under a sun that was no longer an enemy.

Eventually the summons came to entrain for Bombay where, after a journey of several hours, we joined the long queues moving slowly on to the troopship *Franconia*.

1 November 1945

The *Franconia* set sail. We lined the ship's rail looking back on the 'Gateway to India' in silence, each coping with his or her emotional response: some glad to escape from a country where they had felt completely alienated; some with nostalgic memories of people and places; others

NOVEMBER 1945

1945 DECEMBER 1945
S M T W T F S
            1
2 3 4 5 6 7 8
9 10 11 12 13 14 15
16 17 18 19 20 21 22
23 24 25 26 27 28 29
30 31 ... ...

THURSDAY 1

Left Bombay. Ship
not so good
Sent letter to Jim (6)
Worked in ships
hospital.
Dancing in the evening

FRIDAY 2

Wrote to Jim (7)

Worked in ship's
hospital.

A page from the author's pocket diary, 1945.

oblivious to everything but the longing for home and family. A sadness as with the close of some great epic drama settled on my heart.

Very different conditions prevailed on board from those on the outward voyage. There were six women in my cabin on bunks constructed by the ship's carpenter at some stage of the war. Meals were perfunctory affairs with three sittings. It was obviously a matter of getting as many people back home in as short a time as possible, which was what everybody wanted, crew and passengers alike.

Most of the prisoners of war from the Far East had already been repatriated but there were a few who for various reasons were returning in the *Franconia*. I met one of them, a regular army officer, Antony Pender-Cudlip by name, a quiet, fair-haired, slim-figured man who never spoke of his life as a POW. Though I worked with women and children in the ship's hospital in the morning, my evenings were free and I learned to play bridge and liar dice with Tony and his friends. Tony was something of a character. He was frequently to be seen strolling round the deck for exercise, wearing a khaki wool pullover with cotton patches on elbows and shoulders issued by the army to ex-POWs. A brimmed hat of khaki linen, which, he declared, arrived at his prison camp by courtesy of the Australian Red Cross, protected his very fair complexion from the hot sun. He was devoted to his hat, perhaps looking upon it as a symbol of continuity between past and future. At noon he would bring on deck the half-pint of free beer graciously allowed by a concerned government to all ex-prisoners – or so Tony claimed.

I wrote to Jim every day so that he would receive a fine packet of letters from Port Said. Our separation was to last for six months and there was plenty of heartache with letters lost or delayed for weeks, a long patch of illness for Jim after I left and, most exasperating of all, the discovery that a special 'B' release, which would have enabled him to return home in the *Franconia*, had been chasing him all over India.

As we reached the Red Sea the weather turned cold, which caught the women passengers unprepared. We began to think longingly of our warm trousers but a rumour spread that the captain had banned 'slacks' from the decks. Despite the exigencies of the war years, there were still a great many men who did not like women to wear trousers, hoping that a return to peace would mean a return to skirts. I decided to do something about it. I wrote to the captain:

> Dear Sir, the ladies on this 'boat'
>> Can scarce believe their ears!
> I ask you now by common vote
>> To quieten their fears.
>
> You say that slacks may not be worn
>> Upon the deck at nights;
> Dear Sir, this year is 'forty-five',
>> Remember 'Women's Rights!'
>
> Apart from that, a few of us
>> Have no warm clothes but slacks,
> So think again before you tear
>> The garments off our backs.
>
> Up on the decks the wind is high
>> And skirts are most revealing.
> If you were in our shoes – and skirts,
>> Just think how you'd be feeling.
>
> Last but not least, behold the men,
>> Scots kilts are all the rage.
> So why should we not wear the pants?
>> Dear Captain, be your age.

I put the appeal in an envelope and gave it to a steward but there was no reaction from the captain. Before we had time to make an issue of the affair, the weather suddenly changed, the sun came out with a vengeance and we found ourselves passing through the Gulf of Suez.

A blue haze covered the sandstone hills of Arabia; its people in dun-coloured garments as bleached as their camels scarcely showed up against the sand. They moved lazily at the same pace as their laden beasts, seeming to be drugged and dazzled by the staring sun. Slowly the groves of cedar and palm faded into the distance, while over Egypt the sky put on a dramatic orange display to remind us that this was our last sunset of the Orient.

At Tewfik and Suez we picked up more POWs. The following morning a deafening roar awoke us as the vessels on either side hailed our ship as we anchored in Port Said. The vendors of Turkish delight traded from the quay, packets of varying sizes being pulled up to the decks on string. Shortly before eleven o'clock the *Franconia* slipped out of the clamorous port with sirens sounding into the blue water of the Mediterranean.

It was a Sunday, 11 November, Armistice Day. Now we had another war to remember and millions more names to add to the list of those who died because of the paranoia of a few men. A memorial service was held on deck by the captain, which was followed by two minutes' silence. There cannot have been anyone present who didn't have at least one comrade to remember; many of us had scores; a few had hundreds. I called to mind my particular 'Unknown Soldier' of the war, representative of all those I had known who died in the Far East.

It was in Gauhati at the time of the battles of Imphal and Kohima in 1944. I was on night duty. The day sister who handed over to me told me that there was only an Indian orderly in charge of the next ward. 'I've just heard that a dying man has been admitted. Do go and see him as soon as you can,' she said as she signed her report. 'I've been kept so busy that I haven't been able to go across to check.'

After walking round my own ward I went out into the warm Indian night with the bullfrogs keeping up their constant croaking and the fireflies flickering zanily about. I saw a small tent outside and went in. A young man lay unconscious on a camp bed in the last stages of illness. Up till then most of those who had died in my care had been in a row of beds in a ward. I had restrained my emotions for the sake of those who survived, putting on a mask of calm professionalism to hide my feelings. Here there was no one to see. I knelt down by the bedside and wept bitterly, sobbing out all the repressed emotions of the war years. I thought of his parents – his wife perhaps – knowing nothing as yet of the certain death of the one they loved.

After a few minutes I rose and looked for his case history but all it revealed was that he was an American. The doctor must have taken the papers away with him. We seldom admitted Americans to our hospitals as they made their own arrangements. I resolved to find out how he came there, but by the morning I had a high temperature and went down with dengue fever. I heard no more about the dying man. Nevertheless he stayed in my memory and soon after, while the episode was fresh in my mind, I wrote this poem for him.

All men who die in war are in you, soldier.
  Here in this lonely tent
  Sunk in a coma,
With the yelp of jackals falling on deaf ears.

The light from the oil lamp bathes you in shadow.
  No one has come to call
  Bringing you flowers
Nor words of loving hope to calm your fears.

I shed the tears suppressed in crowded wards,
  Fall to my knees to mourn
  The untimely dead,
Who measured life in giving, not in years.

When the service finished and the silent assembly dispersed to their cabins, I remained on deck gazing out to sea. Within a few months I would be a civilian, one amongst thousands adapting to a completely different way of life. Had it not been for the war I would have had little experience of other nationalities and perhaps would never have visited India at all. It was difficult to imagine what aspects of the past would have a lasting influence on the way I thought and acted in the future, yet there were certain attitudes that I was convinced would endure. I would never again put human beings into categories according to race, colour or creed but accept each person on his or her merits; nor would I take for granted good health, a roof over my head and enough to eat for I had seen people deprived of these simple needs for the whole of their short lives.

Now that I had gained sufficient confidence to commit myself to a permanent relationship I would no longer need to savour my most precious recollections in solitude. Henceforth I would be able to share all my memories: musical evenings by the river at Asansol; the intoxicating scent of the frangipani tree in the lane by the sisters' mess; the glowing plumage of the paradise flycatcher in his woodland retreat; dead mango trees where the fruit-bats hung awaiting the coming of night; the feel of monsoon rain on parched skin. And whenever my thoughts grew really gloomy, I could always concentrate on the vision of a little Indian boy playing with a white cat on the deck of a river steamer as it made its way among the sand-banks, safely conducted by the man with the graduated pole.

Index

Abdullah 188, 206
Ackroyd, Lieutenant-Colonel RAMC 102, 108, 114, 115
Adair, Sister M E QAIMNS 112, 119, 120, 129, 143, 162, 208
Amsden, Second Lieutenant R S RE 62, 72
Anrep, Captain I RAMC 156, 157, 164, 174
Arnold, Flying Officer RAF 194
Austin, Major F C K RAMC 82, 83, 100, 102, 108
Aziz, Abdul 151

Bahadur, Abdul 91
Baker, Sister D J ARRC QAIMNS 122, 123, 125, 143, 175, 176, 180
Bamber, Captain J E RA 204, 205
Barber, Captain P RA 204
Basil, Denis 24
Baxter, Captain C RA 199, 200
Bell, Matron E M QAIMNS 42
Bennett-Jones, Captain N RAMC 115, 120, 124, 126
Bevan, Sister QAIMNS 98
Bock, 'Charlie', US Army 149, 152, 171, 174
Bolton, Lieutenant J D P RA 203, 204, 205, 206, 207, 208, 210
Britton, Corporal 100
Brock, Second Lieutenant G M RA 62, 72
Brown, Captain 'Charlie' RA 62, 72
Browne, Dorothy 18, 19, 20, 21
Burgess, Matron A 31, 34, 35, 36, 42
Burton, Second Lieutenant 'Dick' RA 47, 52, 56, 58, 59, 60, 68, 69, 78, 89,
    208

Calder, Ted 161
Cameron, Colonel 127
Cardell, Sister 23, 27, 28
Carton de Wiart, Major-General A VC 49
Cawthorn, Lieutenant-Colonel F R IMS 113, 116, 119, 121, 124, 128, 140,
    170
Cawthorn, Mrs 126
Copping, Sister M E QAIMNS 88
Crawford, Colonel J A RAMC 124, 170
Creas, Mr 133, 134, 135, 136, 137
Creas, Mrs Jeti 134, 135

de Souza, Nurse M 148, 149, 150, 152
Din, Noor 164, 165, 174
Dobbs, Corporal, US Army 100, 101
Dolan, Sister 21, 22

England, Corporal J L REME 188, 189, 190
Evers, Nurse Joan VAD 167

Ferrier, Sister B L QAIMNS 72, 76, 81, 82, 94
Frazer, Sister Ann QAIMNS 195, 208
Freeman, Sister Joyce QAIMNS 180, 186, 207, 208

Gallagher, US Army 184, 188
Graham, Lieutenant 184
Graham-Bower, Ursula 127, 129
Grodd, Captain S RAMC 115, 120, 124, 133
Guggenheim, Sister 16, 18

Hallett, Sister G F QAIMNS 152, 155, 156, 158, 160, 161, 162, 163, 164, 165,
    167, 168, 170, 175, 176, 177, 178, 180, 207, 208
Hamilton, Sister Jean QAIMNS 65, 72
Hargreaves, Lieutenant-Colonel K RA 49, 52, 56, 60, 62, 63, 89
Hennessy, Captain J N RAMC 152, 154, 155, 156, 160, 161, 164, 165, 166,
    167, 169, 170, 171, 176, 177, 178, 188, 207
Herbert, Lady Mary 100, 101
Hind, Mr 74, 75
Hind, Mrs 74, 75
Hobbiss, Major M A H RA 49, 56, 68
Hobley, Sister QAIMNS 42
Horsman, Peter 63
Howard, Brigadier 193
Hughes, Sister 19, 20
Husain, Havildar S I 154, 164, 169, 170

Inman, Sister Joan QAIMNS 112, 116, 132

Jones, Lieutenant 142

Kean, Sister 38
Kearney, Nurse Maura 22, 23, 33, 36
Kenwright, Sister 31, 32
Khan, Abdul 172
Kahn, Budloo 100
King, Sister Mary QAIMNS 88, 112, 119, 140, 141, 142, 143, 193
Kolb, Pilot Officer Hugo RAF 63

Lal, Hari 121, 122
Lamb, Sister Monica QAIMNS 112, 143, 208
Lavender, Captain J RA 194, 195
Lavers, Captain Geoffrey RA 52
Linton, Mr 74, 78
Lossing, Lieutenant-Colonel Edward IMS 76, 78, 81, 82, 84, 85, 86, 87, 90,
    94, 95, 97, 98, 102, 103, 104, 105, 106, 108, 109, 122, 123, 125, 129, 130,
    133, 134, 135, 136, 137, 142, 162, 165, 166, 181, 190, 191, 192, 193, 206
Loughnan, Principal Matron M RRC QAIMNS 129
Lowe, Sergeant 195

Madge, Aunt 14, 15, 16, 26, 29, 40, 42, 87
Magid, Captain 130, 131
Marlsdale, Captain Gerry RA 47, 53
Mayne, Major A W RAMC 145, 150, 161, 162, 175, 176
McKentish, Mr 160, 165, 175, 176

McKenzie, Sister Dora QAIMNS 43, 58, 62
McKenzie, Sister Isobel QAIMNS 43, 58, 62, 112, 130, 133
McLennan, Matron 20, 22
McNally, Sister Mary QAIMNS 65, 72, 73, 74, 75, 78, 79, 80, 82, 85, 92, 95, 98, 99, 208
McQuine, Major 189
Mitchener, Lieutenant F W P RA 47, 53, 58, 59, 69, 78, 89
Mullen, Private 169
Mundell, Captain Geoffrey RA 47, 53, 56, 58, 59, 68
Murray, Captain RAMC 95, 99

Niblock, Mrs Jean 81, 82, 86, 87, 100
Niblock, Major R 81, 82, 86, 87
Niblock, Major W McN IMS 116, 132
Noblet, Barbara 16, 17, 26, 27, 40, 63
Noblet, Winefride 26, 27, 198, 199, 200
Noblet, Thomas Whiteside 13, 14
Nowak, Dr W H 27, 28

Oliver, Sister Doris QAIMNS 43, 44, 46, 50, 58, 62, 63, 65, 66, 70, 88, 112, 133, 138, 140, 143, 162, 180, 208
O'Neill, Lieutenant-Colonel P L IMS 173, 174
Orr, Sister Margaret QAIMNS 44
Owen, Sergeant RAMC 145

Parker, Ross 61
Parker, Mr 98
Parker, Mrs 98
Patterson, Captain RAMC 115
Paxton, Captain John 195
Pearce, Second Lieutenant E RA 47, 58, 59, 60, 68, 69
Pender-Cudlip A E, RA 210
Piggott, Nurse 127
Pilgrim, Sergeant RAMC 145
Pillai, Captain S P K IAMC 146, 149
Pons, Lily 171
Pringle, Sister Marjorie QAIMNS 112, 116
Pushie, Purser R 54

Qerishi, Captain 126
Quinn, Captain P J G RAMC 166, 167

Ramsay, Dr W A 36, 37, 38
Ranking, Major-General R P L 170, 204, 205
Ransome, Lieutenant-Colonel G A IAMC 116, 118, 124, 126, 141, 171
Rennie, Captain 84
Richardson, Anne 22, 23, 30, 31, 34, 35, 36, 81
Ridler, Flight Lieutenant Tony RAF 66
Roberts, Captain T M, Royal Welch Fusiliers 167, 168
Rogerson, Major RAMC 79, 80
Rowan, Captain P M RA 47, 52, 53, 68

Sadler, Captain RAMC 98
Scivea, Sister Eve QAIMNS 168, 176, 180
Scragg, Squadron Leader RAF 194
Sealey, Major Hugh, Frontier Force Rifles 67, 72, 167
Spencer, Captain Lindsay RA 204, 206

Spenlowe, Sister 32
Summerfield, Matron A McC RRC QAIMNS 112, 118, 121, 122, 127, 129, 133, 140, 143

Tobin, Matron E QAIMNS 94, 98, 99, 100, 101, 103
Thompson, Major-General T O RAMC 193, 194
Tuck, Sister G R QAIMNS 98

Udall, Sister F L V QAIMNS 176, 187, 203, 205, 206

Waller, Sister QAIMNS 70, 72, 95
Walter, Florence May 28, 29
Watkins, Private 94, 98, 99
Wells, Charles 25, 26
Wilson, Captain RAMC 79, 80
Wingate, Brigadier Orde 101, 103, 108, 129, 130, 136
Wright, Muriel 41
Wyber, Sister QAIMNS 70, 72, 95
Wylie, Nurse Dorothy VAD 194, 201, 203, 206